Quarterly Essay

1   WITHOUT AMERICA
Australia in the New Asia
Hugh White

82   CORRESPONDENCE
Lyle Shelton, Amy Middleton, Dennis Altman, John Whitehall,
Scott Ryan, Louis Hanson, Benjamin Law

108   Contributors

Quarterly Essay is published four times a year by Black Inc., an imprint of Schwartz Publishing Pty Ltd. Publisher: Morry Schwartz.

ISBN 9781863959636 ISSN 1832-0953

Subscriptions – 1 year print & digital
(4 issues): $79.95 within Australia incl. GST.
Outside Australia $119.95. 2 years print & digital
(8 issues): $149.95 within Australia incl. GST.
1 year digital only: $49.95.

Payment may be made by Mastercard or Visa, or by cheque made out to Schwartz Publishing. Payment includes postage and handling.

To subscribe, fill out and post the subscription card or form inside this issue, or subscribe online:

www.quarterlyessay.com
subscribe@blackincbooks.com
Phone: 61 3 9486 0288

Correspondence should be addressed to:

The Editor, Quarterly Essay
Level 1, 221 Drummond Street
Carlton VIC 3053 Australia
Phone: 61 3 9486 0288 / Fax: 61 3 9011 6106
Email: quarterlyessay@blackincbooks.com

Editor: Chris Feik. Management: Caitlin Yates. Publicity: Anna Lensky. Design: Guy Mirabella. Assistant Editor: Kirstie Innes-Will. Production Coordinator: Hanako Smith. Typesetting: Tristan Main.

Printed in Australia by McPherson's Printing Group. The paper used to produce this book comes from wood grown in sustainable forests.

WITHOUT AMERICA

Australia in the New Asia

Hugh White

For almost a decade now, the world's two most powerful countries have been competing over which of them will dominate the world's most important and dynamic region. America has been trying to remain East Asia's primary power, and China has been trying to replace it. Their contest is playing out over trade deals and infrastructure plans, in the diplomacy of multilateral meetings, and above all through military gamesmanship in regional hotspots like the South China Sea, the East China Sea and the Korean Peninsula. But all these are really just symptoms of their underlying rivalry.

How the contest will proceed – whether peacefully or violently, quickly or slowly – is still uncertain, but the most likely outcome is now becoming clear. America will lose, and China will win. America will cease to play a major strategic role in Asia, and China will take its place as the dominant power. War remains possible, especially with someone like Donald Trump in the Oval Office. But the risk of war recedes as it becomes clearer that the odds are against America, and as people in Washington come to understand that their nation cannot defend its leadership in Asia by fighting an unwinnable war with China. The probability therefore grows that America will peacefully, and perhaps even willingly, withdraw. Indeed, this is already happening, and Asia is changing as a result. The old US-led order is passing, and a new China-led order is taking its place.

This is not what anyone expected. Seven years ago, in Quarterly Essay 39, I argued that as power shifted from Washington to Beijing, and as China's ambitions for leadership in Asia grew, America faced a contest in Asia which it would be unable to win outright. Its best option, therefore, would be to negotiate a new regional order, retaining a lesser but still substantial strategic role in Asia which would balance China's power, limit its influence and prevent East Asia falling under Chinese hegemony.

Many people disagreed. They argued that America's power would remain so much greater than China's that it was unnecessary for America to make any such concessions. By holding firm, it could face down China, convince it to back off and leave American leadership in Asia unchallenged once more.

Alas, my critics and I were both wrong. We were slow to see the growing rivalry between America and China, and we didn't recognise, or permit ourselves to acknowledge, how serious the rivalry has become, and how badly it has been going for America. That is because we all underestimated China's power and resolve, and overestimated America's. Not only is America failing to remain the dominant power, it is failing to retain any substantial strategic role at all. Many expected that China would falter before it grew strong enough to challenge America on anything like equal terms. Instead, China has kept growing stronger, economically, militarily and diplomatically, and America's resolve has weakened. Now it is China that is facing down America. That was the clear message of Xi Jinping's remarkable assertion of China's status and power at the Nineteenth National Congress of the Communist Party of China, in October 2017. The contest is indeed unequal, but not in the way we thought. So we find ourselves in a new Asia, and we do not like it. But that's the hand history is dealing us, and we must make the best of it.

We in Australia haven't seen this coming, because Washington hasn't seen it coming and we have got into the habit of seeing the world through Washington's eyes. We have been happy to accept Washington's assurances that it has China's measure, and Washington itself has been slow to understand how serious China's challenge has become and how badly it has mishandled the contest.

More broadly, our recent history has left us ill-equipped to understand what is happening. The contest between America and China is classic power politics of the harshest kind. We have not seen this kind of struggle in Asia since the end of the Vietnam War, or globally since the end of the Cold War. The generations of politicians, public servants, journalists, analysts and citizens who grew up with power politics and knew how it worked have left the public stage. Political leaders like Menzies and Fraser, Curtin and Whitlam, and Hawke, Keating and Howard; public servants like Arthur Tange; journalists like Peter Hastings and Dennis Warner; academics like Hedley Bull, Tom Millar and Coral Bell; and the voters who lived through the wars and struggles of the first three-quarters of the twentieth century: they would all find Asia today much easier to understand than we do. We have a lot to learn and not much time to learn it.

And of course it has been harder to acknowledge what has been happening in Asia because it has been so difficult to imagine where it is taking us. We are heading for an Asia we have never known before, one without an English-speaking great and powerful friend to dominate the region, keep us secure and protect our interests. The fear that that this might happen – the "fear of abandonment," as Allan Gyngell calls it – has been the mainspring of Australian foreign policy since World War II, and indeed long before. But since the Cold War ended – a generation ago now – we have forgotten those old fears and begun to take American power and protection for granted. We have come to depend more and more on America as its position in Asia has become weaker and weaker.

We have been happy to get rich off China's growth, confident that America can shield us from China's power. Now it is clear that confidence has been misplaced; we need to start thinking for ourselves about how to make our way and hold our corner in an Asia dominated by China.

That is what this essay is about. It looks first at how America is losing the contest with China, and then at Australia: how we have responded to the US–China contest so far, why we have got it so wrong, and what we can do now to manage the new reality we face.

THE SITUATION ROOM

It is 3 a.m. when the President enters the White House Situation Room. "Good morning, everyone. I hope you've all had some sleep. I gather we have a problem. Set the scene for us, will you?" he tells the National Security Adviser.

"Yes, Mr President. Just to bring everyone here up to speed, last week the President warned China not to deploy fighter aircraft to their new base on Mischief Reef in the South China Sea. They had announced they would do that in response to our latest freedom of navigation operations and in the context of our disagreements over North Korea. Over the weekend they defied the President and sent the planes in. Mr President, you were travelling at the time, so there was no chance for lengthy analysis, but you accepted our advice that we could not allow this to stand and ordered Pacific Command to block Chinese sea access to Mischief Reef. PACOM has now got three destroyers in position, and a carrier taskforce is also being rerouted to the area. We announced these steps publicly, and informed the Chinese that their ships approaching Mischief Reef would be intercepted and turned around by our navy. The next day a Chinese navy taskforce escorting a supply ship left Hainan on a course for the reef. Three hours ago they were confronted by our ships. They defied our navy's instructions to turn around. Our commander on the spot was not authorised to use force to stop them. That decision lies with you, sir."

"And what do you advise?"

"Mr President, we really have no choice. Our strategic position in Asia is at stake. America's leadership in Asia depends on the credibility of its threats and promises, and that credibility will be destroyed if we cannot stop the Chinese as we have promised to do."

"That is all quite clear, and I think quite correct." The President turns to the Chairman of the Joint Chiefs of Staff. "Well, General, what are our options?"

"Mr President, on your order we can fire at, and if necessary sink, one of these Chinese ships right away. That is not a problem—"

"So do you agree with the National Security Adviser? Is that what we should do?"

"Not necessarily," the General replies. "We have to consider what would happen next."

"And what would happen next?"

"Well, sir, that is up to the Chinese. They don't want a full-scale war, and they will back off and cut their losses if they think we are willing to let it escalate that far. But we can't assume that's how they'll see it. There is a real chance they think we are bluffing, and that we will be the ones to back off. If they think that, they'll call our bluff and hit us back if we hit them. They could sink our ship, for example."

"And what are the chances they think we are bluffing?" the President asks.

"Hard to say, sir, but the chances are not low. They know we've often drawn Red Lines in the past and not followed through. They probably assume the stakes are lower for us than for them, because it is their backyard. And the stakes for them are very high, so they are probably willing to take some risks. So I'd say the chances of them hitting us back are at least 50/50, probably more."

"But if they do think we are serious this time, and back off after we have fired on their ship, it's a big loss for them and a big win for us."

"Yes, that's right, Mr President. Either way, your decision is a high-stakes bet on how they judge our resolve."

"Okay, so we need to get clear what's at stake if we lose the bet. What happens if we hit them and they hit back?"

"Well, then it would be your turn to decide whether to escalate or back off. Backing off after we had already lost a ship would be even more damaging to our standing in Asia than backing off now. But escalating the conflict further would be a very serious step indeed."

"Of course it would, but I'd be willing to take it if I was sure that we'd win, and win quickly. Can you assure me of that?"

"To be frank with you, Mr President, I cannot. Ten years ago I would have said yes, but today is different. China's military is still much weaker than ours, but they are strong enough to deny us a quick and easy victory in the South China Sea. We would sink a lot of their ships and shoot down a lot of their planes, and we could, if we chose, inflict a lot more damage on them than they could on us. But we would still take serious losses — ships and aircraft, and lives."

"Could we lose a carrier?"

"Sure, if we send it in harm's way. The carriers would be prime targets, and the Chinese have put a lot of money into building the systems to find and sink them. They'd have a fair chance of succeeding."

"Are the Chinese really that good?"

"Well, we're not sure. Their systems and people are quite untested, but combat springs surprises for both sides, most of them unpleasant. It's always a mistake to underestimate your enemy. I think we should expect the Chinese forces to be pretty effective."

"So we might lose thousands? More than in Iraq and Afghanistan?"

"Quite possibly. But the real point is that after a week or two, we might not have landed a decisive blow or achieved a clear outcome that could be presented as a victory. We'd be headed for a stalemate, and a stalemate always looks and feels like defeat."

"Hmm. So what would we do then?"

"By that stage, after suffering significant losses, I think we'd find it very hard to back off, and so would they. So I guess we'd both be inclined to double down. For us that would mean launching a major strike campaign against the bases and facilities on the Chinese mainland which support their air and naval forces. For them it would mean doing the same against our bases in the Western Pacific."

"And where would that end?"

"I don't know, Mr President. We have no real idea of what would count as victory in an escalating conflict against a country as large and powerful as China."

"Okay, understood. But how bad could it get? Could it end up in a nuclear exchange?"

"Mr President, we can't be sure it wouldn't. We don't have a clear idea just where China's nuclear threshold is, and our own thinking about this is much hazier than it was against the Soviets. So we cannot rule it out. And of course that would raise at least the possibility of a Chinese nuclear strike against American cities."

"I see." The President turns again to the National Security Adviser. "Do you still think we have no choice?"

"Well, Mr President, let me rephrase that. We do have a choice. It is a choice between the risk of a serious war — maybe a nuclear war — with China, and the collapse of our strategic leadership in Asia. Whether it is worth risking war to preserve our leadership depends on how important it is to our fundamental national objectives."

The Secretary of State takes a deep breath. "With respect, Mr President, I want to reinforce what the National Security Adviser has said, to make sure we all understand what the decision that you are now contemplating would mean. To be frank, our credibility in Asia has already been badly damaged by our repeated failure to stop the Chinese doing things in the South China Sea that we and our predecessors have called unacceptable. We decided to draw a Red Line around Mischief Reef last week precisely to reassure our allies, and to warn the Chinese, that we would not let things drift any further. To back off again now would therefore massively embolden the Chinese and dismay our allies. They are already worried about our looming vulnerability to North Korean as well as Chinese nuclear attack on our cities. There must come a point at which Japan, especially, loses so much confidence in us that they decide to build their own nuclear forces. If we back off from Mischief Reef now, that point will move much closer. If and when they reach that point, our alliance with Japan is at an end, and with it our role as the primary power in Asia."

"Yes, that's the big question. And here is my answer. The way things look, it is just not clear that leading in Asia, important though it is, justifies the kind of risks we are talking about. General, tell the navy to pull our ships back and let the Chinese pass. I'm not willing to risk a major war."

*

There is not much make-believe about this little scenario. Only two small steps would get us to the situation it depicts: a Chinese decision to deploy combat aircraft, and an American decision to blockade in response. Both steps are quite plausible, having been explicitly canvassed by senior figures in Beijing and Washington, respectively. The issues that are raised as the scenario unfolds, and the choices that the president confronts, are exactly the issues and choices that America would face in an escalating crisis with China. Indeed, in a less acute form they confront decision-makers in Washington every day as they jostle with China over many issues in Asia. Some in Washington now understand that, as this poignant snippet from the *New York Times* last year makes clear:

> "Would you go to war over Scarborough Shoals?" General Dunford asked Admiral Harris, in a conversation overheard by a reporter. If Admiral Harris responded, it could not be heard.

Understanding the issues and choices that US decision-makers face is the key to understanding why America is losing its primacy in Asia, and the best way to do that is to explore the interplay of power, interests and resolve that underpins this Situation Room scenario. To do that, we have to enter the murky milieu of power politics.

Power politics is what happens when strong states – great powers – compete for influence and authority. It doesn't happen all the time, because often, and sometimes for decades on end, most countries know and accept their place in the international pecking order. Nineteenth-century Europe was like that, and Asia since 1972 has been too. But there are times when assumptions about power and influence – about who sets the international rules and who must follow them – are challenged, and the old order is overturned. That happens especially when the distribution of power shifts among great powers, with some getting stronger and others becoming at least relatively weaker. The rising powers try to grab more influence and authority, and the declining powers struggle to hold on to the influence they have. Then power politics kicks in, as great powers compete for influence and authority in the new international order that emerges to replace the old one.

The stakes in these contests are very high. Great powers care deeply about their place in the international system, because everything else that is most important to them – their security, prosperity and status – depends on it. Only the direct defence of their own land and people matters more to them, and often not even that. That is why so many of the biggest wars in history have been fought over power and status, and why armed force is so central to power politics. Contests between rising and declining powers do not inevitably end in war, but they have always been the main cause of major wars between great powers, and the possibility of major conflict permeates every element of power politics and determines the outcome of the contest, whether a war eventuates or not.

That is because a country's willingness to go to war, or rather its ability to convince others that it is willing to go to war, determines its place in the international system. The conduct of power politics – the positioning and posturing – is all about establishing what issues the contestants for power are willing to go to war over. So, for example, the order in nineteenth-century Europe was defined by the evident willingness of all the great powers to go to war to preserve the balance of power among them. That is what persuaded them all to uphold the status quo for so long – until 1914.

Many people hoped that the nuclear age would put an end to this kind of power politics, but the Cold War showed otherwise. The threat of nuclear war seems only to have raised the stakes, not changed the game. In the nuclear age, everyone seems more confident that their rivals won't risk a conflict, without becoming any less confident that their rivals still believe they will. So the international order of Cold War Europe was defined by the evident willingness of both the Soviets and the Americans to go to war with one another to prevent any intrusion by the other into their respective spheres of influence, in Eastern and Western Europe. And the US-led order in Asia since the 1970s was defined by the evident unwillingness of any Asian power to risk war with America to challenge its leading position, and America's equally evident willingness to go to war to resist any challenge.

*

Asia became largely free of power politics in 1972, when China stopped challenging America in the region. Now the power politics has returned because China has reversed course and started to challenge America again, and the two countries confront one another in a classic contest between a rising power that wants to take over the regional leadership and a declining power that wants to hold on to it.

Which country ends up as the leading power in Asia will depend on the issues they can each convince the other they are prepared to fight over. To preserve its leadership, America must convince China that it is willing to go to war to resist China's challenge. That doesn't mean it has actually to fight a war, only that it must convince China that it is willing to do so. China has to show that it is willing to fight to depose the United States. It is doing this now by the classic power-political ploy of salami-slicing. The aim is to test America's resolve over a series of issues of little intrinsic worth, which on the face of it do not seem worth fighting over. But while each slice of the salami might be insignificant, Washington looks weak if it can't or won't stop China taking one slice after another, and China by contrast looks strong and resolved. This undermines the credibility of US leadership, as regional countries lose confidence that Washington will support them if the next slice of the salami is them. China's influence is correspondingly enhanced, as its neighbours grow less willing to defy it.

This is what's happening in the South China Sea today. It has very little to do with questions of sovereignty over reefs and rocks, or who has rights over which areas of ocean. Nor does it have much to do with arcane questions of international law. These substantive questions merely provide the setting for Washington and Beijing to display their strategic resolve, and to put their rival's to the test. By deploying their militaries to the contested area, both America and China are signalling their willingness to use force to win the point and to demonstrate that the other is not. America has hoped to show that China will back off rather than risk a confrontation, and China hopes to show that it will be America that backs off. This is pure power politics at work. And so far, China is winning.

Of course, neither side wants a clash, let alone a major war, because both understand that even so great a prize as leadership in Asia would not be worth such a massive disaster. But that doesn't stop them playing power politics, because each side believes it can get what it wants without a war, because the other will retreat to avoid one. The Chinese seem convinced that America will surrender regional leadership rather than risk a war with China, and the Americans have been equally sure, at least until recently, that China will drop its challenge and go back to accepting US leadership rather than risk a war with America.

Sometimes this kind of gamesmanship works: one side or the other decides the game is not worth the candle and backs off, or each side comes to accept the other's key interests and they reach a modus vivendi. That is why war is not inevitable between a rising power and an established power. The idea that it is – that an iron law of history dictates rising powers always fight established rivals, so that China must end up at war with America – has been about for many years, and has been expertly analysed recently by American political scientist Graham Allison. A famous line in Thucydides' account of the Peloponnesian War is often mistranslated to say that the rising power of Athens challenging the established power of Sparta made war "inevitable." In fact, Thucydides' subtle and elusive Greek expressed a much more sophisticated and accurate judgment: that the rivals were trapped in a situation which made it hard for them to escape war.

History bears this out. War might not be inevitable, but it is a very serious risk. Even when neither side wants war, miscalculations can easily happen. Each side tends to assume that its resolve is stronger than its rival's, so is tempted to push ahead into a confrontation, believing the other will back off. Then the confrontation escalates, the rhetoric intensifies, and the stakes grow as the costs of backing down increase. Each side can quite quickly reach the point where backing down looks worse than going to war, and a war starts which no one wants.

That is what happened in 1914. People often talk about the obvious parallels between Europe then and Asia today, as a rising power confronts a long-established leader. But the more important parallel is less obvious. War came in the last week of July 1914, when decision-makers in the key capitals — Vienna, St Petersburg and Berlin — believed they could prevail over their rivals because they assumed their opponents would back down. But they were all wrong: no one backed down, and by the time that became clear, each power was too committed to step back. They all reluctantly went to war because the national humiliation of retreating at that late stage appeared even worse.

This is the danger we face in Asia today: that both Washington and China, neither of them wanting war but each underestimating the other's resolve, will allow a crisis to escalate to the point where they each face a disastrous choice between war and humiliation, and both choose war, just as Europe's leaders did a century ago. In our Situation Room scenario, war is averted because the President decides to relinquish America's strategic position in Asia, but we can see how easily the choice could have gone the other way. The key point is that in this kind of contest, countries are almost certain to face that kind of choice, as America could do almost any day. If it is not willing to fight, it must back down, and wars often happen because backing down is so hard.

The power of a country like the United States does not disappear overnight, but leadership is not just about raw power. It requires evident resolve to use that power, and to use it deftly and effectively, and that can be fatally damaged by a swift blow from which there is no recovery. A single crisis, not necessarily very important in itself, often marks the point at which the loss of a waning power's authority, hitherto only half-acknowledged, becomes inescapably clear to friend and foe alike. Everyone's assumptions and expectations then change. Rivals realise they need no longer fear the waning power, and friends understand they can no longer depend on it. When this happens, it becomes quite suddenly impossible to continue as before, because elements of the international order that depended on the waning power's authority quickly collapse. Alliances crumble as countries lose faith in once-trusted security commitments, subordinate powers start to act more independently, and ambitious powers flex their muscles as the constraints that have held them back start to fray. This is what happened when the Soviets abandoned Afghanistan, and when the British humiliated themselves in the Suez Crisis of 1956.

There is a strong chance that Donald Trump will face a crisis like the one in the Situation Room while he is president. It might not be over the South China Sea. It could be over the Senkaku/Diaoyu Islands in the East China Sea, or over Taiwan, or North Korea. But the probability that he will face it somewhere is high, because Beijing has been deliberately creating situations in some of these flashpoints to test America's resolve, and it will keep doing so. So far these provocations have worked well for Beijing because Washington has made no effective response, and that has allowed China to win by default. With deft diplomacy President Obama mostly avoided situations where the choice was too stark, but in doing so he largely abandoned the field to China anyway. For as long as Washington follows Obama's example and avoids a confrontation with China by doing nothing effective to deter Beijing from taking another slice of salami, its strategic position in Asia will continue to erode. If instead it pushes back hard, it will spark a confrontation and face the tough choice in the Situation Room between war and the swift collapse of its leadership in Asia. The only escape is to hope China backs off, and that looks less and less likely every day.

*

The strategic trends in Asia have been running against America ever since China began seriously to challenge it in about 2008. Washington's response was President Obama's "Pivot to Asia," launched in 2011, which has failed. Exploring how and why it failed will help us better understand the nature of the challenge that America faces and why a more effective response is so hard to find.

The Pivot aimed to deter Beijing from challenging US leadership by affirming America's determination to remain Asia's primary power. "The United States is a Pacific power, and we are here to stay," Obama said, declaring that America would defend this status "with every element of American power. So let there be no doubt: In the Asia-Pacific in the twenty-first century, the United States of America is all in."

These were fine words, but they were not enough. The Pivot failed because there was almost nothing more to it than this declaration of intent. No substantial commitment of resources backed it up. The modest measures that were announced under the Pivot banner, like the deployment of US marines to Darwin, were no more than symbolic gestures to underline the message. They did not constitute a tangible deployment of national power on anything like the scale needed to counter a serious challenge by the world's second-most powerful state for leadership of the world's most prosperous and dynamic region. They did nothing to reverse the shift in relative power in China's favour. Instead these weak measures undermined rather than reinforced the Pivot's intended message, by showing how little America was really willing to do to buttress its position in Asia.

There was a simple reason for this major miscalculation. The architects of the Pivot in the Obama administration, and indeed the bulk of the US foreign-policy establishment, did not take China's challenge seriously. They assumed that China had neither the power to confront America as a strategic rival, nor the ambition to take its place as the leading regional power. That led them to assume that China's increasingly assertive behaviour was really just a try-on. They convinced themselves that America's long post-9/11 preoccupation with the Middle East had misled Beijing into thinking that America was no longer committed to leadership in Asia. All that was necessary, therefore, was to correct Beijing's mistake by reaffirming America's commitment, and China would swiftly and quietly back off.

One can see why this line of thinking appealed in Washington. If it was true, America would be able to stay on top in Asia without incurring major costs or running serious risks. There would be no danger of war, because China would not dream of risking a confrontation with America which might lead to an armed clash. Relations with Beijing, which were so important to the US economy and in addressing key global issues like climate change, would not be affected. And America's friends and allies, including Australia, would be reassured that they could support US leadership in Asia without endangering their own relations with China. No one would have to choose between the two countries.

Alas, Washington's assumptions were all wrong. China's challenge was deadly serious, and in March 2012, a few months after President Obama launched the Pivot in Canberra, Beijing's leaders seized an opportunity to demonstrate this. They staged a test of Washington's resolve, to see whether President Obama really was ready to commit "every element of American power" to preserve the US position in Asia. They seized Scarborough Shoal in the South China Sea from the Philippines, and flouted a deal brokered by America to defuse the situation. This challenged America's credibility at several levels: as an ally of the Philippines, as the region's preponderant naval power, and as the arbiter of regional order. When Washington quietly declined Manila's request for the US Navy to help push the Chinese out, Beijing's point was plainly made. It would not be deterred by Obama's fine words. It was serious about contesting US leadership in Asia, and was willing to defy Washington and risk a confrontation to do so. Beijing gambled that it would be Washington that would shy away from the possibility of confrontation, and the bet paid off.

This has set the pattern for events in the Western Pacific ever since. Later in 2012, Beijing extended its tactics to the East China Sea, using military and paramilitary deployments to contest Japan's control of the disputed Senkaku/Diaoyu Islands, and testing America's willingness to risk a confrontation in support of its Tokyo ally. Then, in 2014, Beijing started to build bases on islands and features in the South China Sea, including Mischief Reef, which were claimed by other countries, including US allies. This took its provocations to a new level, and posed an even starker test of America's resolve. Parts of the Obama administration, especially the Pentagon and Pacific Command in Hawaii, saw this as a chance to draw a Red Line and compel China to stop. They raised the ante, hoping to rally support among China's neighbours and globally by highlighting the threat that its provocations posed to the international law of the sea and freedom of navigation. They took heart when, in July 2016, the Permanent Court of Arbitration in The Hague ruled against China's claims in the South China Sea. And they initiated a series of freedom of navigation operations by US naval ships through Chinese-claimed waters to contest China's claims.

But none of this made any difference to China. Washington's diplomatic initiatives were blunted when the Philippines, which was most directly affected by Beijing's provocations, joined other Southeast Asian countries in refusing to take sides against China. Some openly sided with Beijing, others sat on the fence, and even those who supported Washington's criticisms were careful to do nothing that would damage their relations with Beijing.

The freedom of navigation operations succeeded in asserting abstruse points of international law, but failed to stop China from building its bases, and the cautious, low-key and legalistic way they were conducted only emphasised how reluctant Washington was to do anything that might risk a confrontation or disrupt the wider relationship with China. The result was therefore quite counterproductive for Washington. Its leaders hoped to show that they could inflict enough pain on Beijing to make it back off, and they failed. Instead they showed that they were not will-ing to bear the pain that China could inflict on them. Washington ended up accepting things that it had called unacceptable, thereby showing that it was America, not China, that would back off from a confrontation. This was precisely the opposite of what the Pivot was supposed to achieve.

These diplomatic and strategic setbacks were amplified by failures in the economic wing of the Pivot. The Obama administration tried to use the Trans-Pacific Partnership (TPP) to reaffirm America's commitment to Asia and counteract the gravitational pull of China's economy, by forging a new and far-reaching trade deal that would exclude China and help restore America's place as Asia's key economic partner. This never made much sense, either economically or strategically. China's place at the cen-tre of Asia was assured by its sheer scale and the depth of its integration with the economies of its neighbours. Nothing the TPP achieved could displace China as the principal source of future economic opportunities for countries throughout Asia. That meant the TPP would do little to reduce China's leverage over its neighbours, or to make them more likely to align with Washington against Beijing. It was plainly overshadowed by China's much bigger and more enticing economic agenda, including the Asian Infrastructure Investment Bank and the Belt and Road Initiative. So the TPP would have done nothing to help Washington strategically, had it succeeded. But by promoting it as a test of US resolve and commitment in Asia, the Obama administration ensured that there would be a lot of dam-age when it was dumped – not just by Donald Trump, but by one of its architects, Hillary Clinton.

By the time Obama left office it was clear the Pivot had failed. In the five years since its announcement, China's challenge to US primacy in Asia had become more direct and overt, and America had found no way to deter it from pushing further and harder. America's allies and friends in Asia had lost confidence in its leadership as a result. Whoever won the election on 8 November 2016 would therefore have faced a big problem in trying to reassert US leadership in Asia. The Democratic candidate, Hillary Clinton, campaigned on a commitment to try. Not so the man who won.

As a candidate, Donald Trump rejected the whole idea of American global leadership, which had been the orthodoxy on both sides of the political divide for generations, and he dismissed America's key alliances globally, and in Asia. He seemed perfectly comfortable with strategic withdrawal from the region. His focus was on trade, and his promise to wage a trade war with China suggested that he would be content to see America's economic stake in Asia dwindle too. As president-elect, he seemed to wax tougher on China when he questioned America's acceptance of the One China policy, but in office he has been distinctly conciliatory and accommodating. His senior officials have tried to reassure Asian allies that America remains committed to them, but that is belied by the wider pattern of events. The Pivot was quietly but firmly dumped a few weeks after Trump's inauguration, and nothing so far has replaced it, leaving America without any kind of settled policy on China or on America's place in Asia. Notable China hawks in Trump's retinue have been sidelined, the rhetoric on trade has softened, and the new administration has gone out of its way to emphasise cooperation with Beijing. Trump has spoken warmly about Xi Jinping, especially after their meeting at Mar-a-Lago in April 2017, and has been disappointed rather than angry that Beijing has not done more against North Korea. The Chinese, for their part, seem to have worked out how to play Trump to their advantage, paying little attention to his bluster and never directly criticising him.

The result is that, under Trump, America seems to have abandoned the objective of resisting China's challenge in Asia. Washington no longer criticises China the way it did; nor does it promote its own vision of Asia's future, in opposition to China's. The South China Sea seems to have slipped quietly down Washington's agenda, and US Navy freedom of navigation operations have been repackaged as routine and low-key. Indeed, the administration has scarcely acknowledged that America faces a strategic contest with China in Asia. The trend in Washington seems clear. Trump is not committed to maintaining US leadership in Asia. He is content to see America's influence in the region wane while China's grows. We shouldn't be surprised. Trump as president is doing what he said he'd do in his campaign. This is "America First" in action. He just doesn't see why Americans should pay to shield China's neighbours from China's power. He thinks they should look after themselves.

Of course, that is only one side of the Trump phenomenon. The other side is the blustering, thin-skinned, erratic egocentric who seems perfectly capable of taking America to war on a whim. We should not take this danger lightly. There has never been an American president so prone to massive errors of judgment on matters great and small. Indeed, there has probably never been such an erratic and irresponsible decision-maker in command of nuclear weapons anywhere since the nuclear age began. And there is no reason to be confident that cooler and wiser heads lower down the chain of command would countermand a catastrophic order and save us from disaster.

This presents a conundrum. Donald Trump is much less likely than his predecessors to start a war with China to defend America's position as the leading power in Asia. Yet he seems much more likely to start a war for no good reason at all. So far, fortunately, he has shown no sign of wanting to start a war with Beijing, but Pyongyang is in his sights.

Trump inherited a failed policy on North Korea. America has been trying to stop North Korea becoming a nuclear power for decades. But negotiations always foundered on the fact that there is nothing America can offer North Korea that its rulers want more than nuclear weapons. Sanctions will not work as long as Beijing is unwilling to bring the regime in Pyongyang to its knees, and there is no credible military option. North Korea's nuclear and missile programs are widely dispersed, well hidden and protected in deep tunnels. That means they can't be seriously damaged by a few airstrikes. Only a full-scale invasion and occupation would be sure to find and destroy Pyongyang's nuclear capability completely, and that has never been an option. America has therefore had no choice but to watch on as North Korea acquired nuclear weapons and the means to deliver them. But no one in Washington wanted to acknowledge this uncomfortable fact, so they have just kept kicking the can down the road, declaring their determination to eliminate North Korea's nuclear and missile forces but doing nothing effective about it.

As luck would have it, Trump has become president just as Pyongyang is moving beyond small-yield warheads and medium-range missiles to develop much bigger thermonuclear weapons and intercontinental ballistic missiles (ICBMs) that could hit US cities. This means Pyongyang could launch an unprovoked nuclear attack on America itself, but the certainty of massive US retaliation makes that extremely unlikely. The bigger issue is what North Korean ICBMs mean for Japan and South Korea. They already live under the shadow of North Korea's shorter-range nuclear forces, but they have been confident that US extended nuclear deterrence – the threat of massive retaliation following an attack on an American ally – would deter Pyongyang from using them. But that confidence is collapsing as North Korea's ICBMs give it the capacity to hit US cities, because Washington's threat to retaliate becomes less credible once Pyongyang can threaten nuclear counter-retaliation against America. Tokyo and Seoul then have to think about getting nuclear weapons of their own to deter North Korea directly, and if they do that their alliances with America would be gravely weakened, if not destroyed, which in turn would shatter America's wider strategic position in Asia.

President Obama saw this as a real danger, which is why he warned Donald Trump that North Korea's ICBMs were the most urgent problem he would face on moving into the Oval Office. Trump probably sees it differently. He no doubt meant what he said last year when he suggested that Japan and South Korea should get their own nuclear weapons, because it fits perfectly with his long-held view that America doesn't need its allies. And even he must understand that an unprovoked North Korean attack on US soil is extremely unlikely. So what is driving his flamboyantly vitriolic campaign against Pyongyang? The most likely answer is that he thinks it makes him look good, and plays well to his base. This is the other side of Trump's "America First." It is not just about stepping back and letting others deal with problems that don't threaten America directly. It is also about stepping forward to crush anyone who does threaten America directly. Or at least appearing willing to do so. Trump's model of American politics requires him to look utterly ruthless in dealing with America's enemies, and North Korea has so far offered him a chance to do just that. For him that probably means much more than any strategic argument about the consequences of North Korean ICBMs.

How far will he take this? There is no doubt that he would attack North Korea if North Korea attacked America or its allies, and he might well be justified in doing so. That is why Pyongyang is unlikely to do anything so foolish. The scarier possibility is that Trump launches a pre-emptive war to deprive the North of its nuclear weapons, which he has plainly threatened to do. That would probably escalate quickly into the biggest and costliest war that America has seen since Vietnam or Korea, and perhaps much bigger than either of those. It could easily become a nuclear war. So how worried should we be?

Clearly there is a real danger that Trump will feel compelled to make good on his buffoonish threats. But the danger may be lower than it appears, because neither Trump nor his political supporters back home seem to care much about the disconnection between what he says and what he does, on foreign policy or anything else. Normal political leaders don't make the kind of threats Trump makes, because they are so anxious to preserve their credibility. When they find themselves in a tight corner, they will go to extremes, including going to war, to avoid being seen to back down. Trump genuinely doesn't seem to care about such things, so he probably won't mind, and maybe won't even notice, if his bluff is called by the North Koreans.

That is something to be grateful for, but it comes at a cost. Trump may not care about the credibility of the threats and promises he makes in America's name, but others do. The way things are going, the most likely outcome is that, for all his tough talk, Trump finds he can do nothing to stop North Korea's ICBM program, and yet again America will look weak as it ends up tolerating something that it had earlier declared to be intolerable. That will strike another very serious blow to America's strategic credibility and amplify the damage already done by the failure of the Pivot. Every time America's leaders issue empty threats, its rivals are emboldened, its allies are discouraged and its leadership is weakened.

Nor is the damage limited to the North Korea issue. Trump's foolish talk of war undermines American power and influence more broadly. At home it weakens his ability to unite Americans behind tough decisions if and when they are needed. Abroad it dismays US allies and friends. It makes them both more worried that he will get them into a war without good reason, and less confident that he will support them when they need it. It amplifies the uncertainties created by his strange relations with Russia, his disdain for European allies and his muddled approach to the Middle East. The damage goes beyond Trump. The evident inability of the Washington foreign-policy and defence establishments to stop Trump making a fool of himself, let alone nudge him towards realistic policies, further undermines their credibility, already badly damaged by decades of strategic failure, especially in the Middle East. Rex Tillerson has proved to be the worst secretary of state in living memory, and the overpraised General James Mattis in Defense has failed to bring coherence to the administration's strategy. Trump has found it easy to sideline, bypass or ignore the experts, and the experts have found it hard to convince anyone that they have the answers that America needs anyway. The authority and credibility of the policy establishment is at its weakest when America needs it most. It became harder and harder under Bush and Obama for US friends and allies to believe that America was a country whose strength, resolve and statecraft they could rely on. Under Trump it becomes almost impossible.

*

While America's problems in Asia are not Donald Trump's fault alone, it is clear that he and his team are making things a lot worse. We are in danger of becoming accustomed to the absurdities of this White House, and resigned to the serious damage that Trump and those around him are doing to the fabric of US politics, government and society. But we should not allow our growing familiarity with his failings to dull our sense of bewilderment and dismay that a person so utterly unfit for the office, morally, intellectually and temperamentally, should have been elected president of the United States. He is plainly very egocentric, but the extent of this egocentricity remains hard to grasp. His outsized sense of himself leaves no room in his consciousness for the state or the society that he leads. He seems to have no concept of the state itself as a great collective enterprise with interests and objectives beyond his own. It really is all about him, so he speaks and acts simply for himself, not so much reckless about as quite unconscious of the consequences for the country he is supposed to lead. And what matters for him is how he feels about himself and how he thinks others feel about him, so he says and does whatever appeals to him, and what he thinks will appeal to others at the moment he says it. So he talks of war, it seems, not with any thought of what war might cost or what it might achieve, but simply because he likes the way he sounds when he talks this way, and thinks others will like it too. That such a person could have been elected president of the United States is one of the strangest events in the history of representative government. That he was elected at this time, when America faces such challenges in Asia, makes the future of American power there all the more precarious.

Of course Trump will pass, but perhaps not till 2024. By then, on current trends, America's place in the world and in Asia will be changed forever. Even if he goes in 2020, or fails to serve a full term, he will have done irreparable harm to US leadership. But more important still, we have to ask who will follow him, and how they will see America's future role. The deep gulf that Trump's election revealed between Washington's political and policy elites and the country at large is nowhere wider and deeper than in foreign policy. Before last year's election it seemed that America, bitterly divided as it was on so many issues, was at least united in supporting the vision of American global leadership that had emerged at the end of the Cold War. The essentials of that vision were broadly bipartisan, uniting politicians across the spectrum, from mainstream Democrats like Hillary Clinton to conservative Republicans like John McCain. All agreed that America must do whatever it took to remain the preponderant power globally and in key regions. It was an unchallengeable axiom of US politics that no one could be elected president without committing to that vision.

Last year's election showed that this was wrong. It revealed that a lot of Americans care very little about US global leadership, and not only those who voted for Trump. On the other side of politics, Bernie Sanders built a huge following in the 2016 Democratic primaries on a platform which repudiated the orthodox vision of America's place in the world almost as starkly as Trump's did. Perhaps most strikingly, Barack Obama, in his last year as president, also turned against the received wisdom about US global responsibilities. In a remarkable interview with the *Atlantic*'s Jeffrey Goldberg, Obama mocked what he called the "Washington playbook" of America's foreign-policy establishment, and defended his decisions to step America back from the roles and responsibilities that so many others in Washington take for granted.

So we have to ask ourselves whether the old consensus about US leadership is gone forever. There will always be candidates who argue, as

Trump does, that America should be quick to strike anyone who threatens America directly. But it is hard to see future candidates blithely assuming that America should keep the world safe for everyone else as well, and it is hard to see them winning many votes if they do. Presidential hopefuls in 2020 and beyond are much more likely to follow Trump and Sanders by promising to step back from international commitments, rather than stepping up to them. Trump is just a symptom of this tectonic shift in America's vision of itself, and it is perhaps the deepest reason to doubt that US leadership in Asia can last much longer. It is worth exploring why and how this has happened.

*

Over the four decades of the Cold War, America's purpose in Asia was clear. Preventing the spread of communism in East Asia was key to the containment of the Soviet Union, and America committed immense resources to the task. It built major alliances, accepted heavy obligations, deployed vast forces and fought two major wars, in Korea and Vietnam. But that purpose evaporated when the Soviet Union collapsed, and for a while it was far from clear whether any new purpose would take its place. Few people assumed that America's interests in Asia after the Cold War required it to keep bearing the costs and risks that it had carried for so long to contain the Soviet threat. In those years Americans were unsure of their economic future, and eager to shed their global burdens. Bill Clinton captured this mood and defeated George Bush Senior in 1992 with the slogan "It's the economy, stupid."

But by the middle of the decade America had decided to stay on in Asia as the region's leading power. Three factors bore on that decision. First, America's economic anxieties were replaced by a buoyant confidence in its future wealth and power. This was the time when people started to talk of America not just as the world's sole superpower, but as a new kind of global power, a "hyperpower." It seemed endowed with unchallengeable global preponderance in every dimension of national strength – economic, technological, military, diplomatic and ideological. It became a cliché to compare America's power with Rome's at its height. America's abundant wealth and power meant that it could easily afford the costs of leading Asia.

Second, it became clear that with the Soviets gone, America's leadership in Asia would cost very little, because it now faced no major rivals. Japan had succumbed to economic stagnation and no longer posed the challenge that some had feared in the 1980s. In the mid-1990s China barely registered as an economic or strategic competitor, and no one foresaw how swiftly that would change. Almost every country in Asia was eager for close relations with America and welcomed its leading role. Only the North Koreans remained plainly hostile, and even they had recently bowed to US pressure and agreed (or pretended to agree for a time) to abandon their nuclear program. All this meant that leadership in Asia would be cheap.

Third, by the mid-1990s America had discovered a new vision of itself. It had emerged as the undisputed leader of a new global order. This new order was accepted and supported by all the world's other major powers, and would extend to every region. It embodied American principles and values, and was upheld and defended by American power. It represented the end of history and made great-power rivalry and power politics a thing of the past. It represented a final and irreversible victory for free trade, market economics, liberal-democratic politics and American military power. It was an intoxicating vision, and not by any means ignoble. Americans seized on it eagerly and happily accepted the burdens involved in maintaining it. That was in large part because they assumed these burdens would be very light indeed. Who, after all, would want to oppose such an appealing global vision for the new century, and who would dare confront American power? Everyone assumed that America's military could defeat any enemy, anywhere, without serious cost, so it need fear no rival.

It is hard, now, to recall this vision without sounding sarcastic about its naivety, after all that has happened over the past two decades and with what is happening in America today. But what is surprising is not how fragile and illusory it has turned out to be, but how, notwithstanding all the setbacks, it has retained its grip for so long, and still so powerfully shapes the perceptions and expectations of policy-makers and analysts in Washington and beyond. The post–Cold War ideal of a unified global order led by America has been the foundation of the Washington foreign-policy orthodoxy that Donald Trump has so recently overturned, and it still guides a lot of thinking in Washington – and elsewhere, including Canberra – about what America can and should do, globally and in Asia. So it is worth asking what happened to it.

The first shock was 9/11, but that strengthened rather than weakened the appeal of global leadership, because it was so easy to conclude from the 9/11 attacks that America's own security depended on bringing all parts of the world to recognition of America's power and acceptance of its principles. The tougher test came in the War on Terror that followed, and especially the invasion of Iraq. The invasion was supposed to show America's power at work. The Bush administration's neoconservatives believed that American armed force could bring Iraq, and then the wider Middle East, to accept US leadership. But they were wrong, and the invasion instead showed the limits of American power and resolve. It disembowelled Iraq, empowered Iran and helped spark the Arab Spring, which led to the dismemberment of Syria and the collapse of US influence in the region.

It fell to Barack Obama to work out what to do about all this. Washington's foreign-policy establishment urged him to restore US influence by re-engaging more deeply, especially in Syria. They argued that this was critical to rebuilding America's position in the Middle East, which in turn was essential to preserving the vision of a US-led global order. But Obama refused. He argued that effective action would require a massive commitment, which American interests would not justify and American voters would not support. The logic of his position was plain: if US global leadership required that kind of commitment to the Middle East, then the price was too high. This reasoning was clearest in his decision not to enforce the Red Line on Syria's use of chemical weapons in 2013, but it informed everything he did in the region. And while the foreign-policy establishment criticised him, he met no serious resistance from either side of Congress. America's influence in the Middle East is now lower than at any time since World War II.

US global leadership faced its second test in Eastern Europe. It was assumed in Washington that Russia would allow itself to be drawn into America's global order through integration with a unified Europe. Instead, Russia has set out to build its own sphere of influence, contesting the post–Cold War redrawing of its western borders, and resisting the spread of Western and European ideas among its neighbours. Moscow's 2008 intervention in Georgia, the seizure of Crimea and its intrusions into eastern Ukraine are all part of this pattern, and they directly challenged America's strategic leadership in Europe.

Again, Obama had to decide what to do. Again, much of America's foreign-policy establishment urged him to push back decisively to defend and uphold the vision of a US-led global order. Again, Obama refused to take any steps which might risk a major and costly commitment, and especially any steps which might lead to war with Russia. As a result, America's power and authority in Europe has been undermined. The myth of American military invincibility, punctured in Iraq and Afghanistan, suffered another sharp correction when it became clear that America had no credible military options to confront Russia on or near Russia's own borders. Obama was not going to risk a war with Moscow to defend the foreign-policy establishment's vision of European order and US global leadership, and few in Congress or beyond the Beltway seemed to think he was wrong.

That vision's third test has been China's challenge to America's leadership in Asia, which only really materialised while Obama was president. As we have seen, he responded differently to this test. He believed, or was convinced by his advisers, that America's leadership could be preserved in Asia at an acceptable cost, because China could easily be deterred. That was what the Pivot was supposed to do. Perhaps he believed also that if the Pivot worked and America remained the leader of Asia, it would preserve its leadership globally, despite setbacks in the Middle East and Eastern Europe, because Asia was the world's most important region. But the Pivot did not work, and America instead finds itself losing a contest with China for leadership in Asia.

So the post–Cold War world has turned out very differently from the heady vision of the mid-1990s. In fact the last two decades have seen an almost unbroken record of US failure to achieve any of the strategic objectives it set itself. Those objectives have included peace between Israel and the Palestinians, preventing Iran and North Korea from getting nuclear weapons, stabilising Iraq and Afghanistan, reconciling Russia to its post-Soviet status, and resisting China's ambitions in Asia. None of these has been achieved, except in part and temporarily in Iran, and the cost of some of these failures, especially in Iraq and Afghanistan, has been immense. So it is not surprising that Americans have turned their back on it, first under Obama, and now, in bizarrely different style, under Trump.

Trump is unique and unprecedented, but he is not necessarily an aberration. His presidency is the product of trends in American politics and society, and its place in the world, stretching back decades, and it may be that his extreme nature reflects the failure of the US system to acknowledge and adapt to those shifts more effectively and sooner. In a way, Trump, in his braggadocio and confusion and fantasies, is the embodiment of a nation deeply ill-at-ease with itself and with the image of its place in the world.

Despite the failure of the Pivot, there is still a lot of wishful thinking in Washington about China. Too many people there think that the best course is to wait for it to collapse, economically, politically and diplomatically. That is a big mistake. Washington will never find an effective response to China's challenge until it acknowledges how fast and how far power has shifted China's way.

Many people continue to believe that the Chinese economy is not nearly as big as the statistics suggest, and is on the brink of a collapse so severe that it will restore American primacy and eliminate China's challenge. This is a fantasy. China's economy has huge problems – structural, demographic, institutional and technological – and it will no doubt suffer major setbacks, as all economies do. It may well stagnate and even shrink for a while. But the economy that has been built since 1980 is real, and will not simply disappear. That means the radical shift in global distribution of wealth and power brought about by China's rise will not be reversed. China's GDP has already overtaken America's on some measures, and is on track to overtake it on any measure within a decade. Accountancy firm PwC estimates that it will exceed America's by 40 per cent in 2030. Even if that's wrong – even if China's economy stopped growing today – it is already far bigger, relative to America's, than the Soviet economy ever was. So China does not need to grow further to be wealthy and strong enough to challenge America in Asia. But it is only prudent to anticipate that China will keep growing, will soon become the world's largest economy however it is measured, and, since wealth is the foundation of power, the world's most powerful state. That is what America, and the rest of us, must learn to deal with.

Likewise, many people believe that China's challenge will evaporate because the Chinese Communist Party's grip on power is about to slip. It is true that the Party faces huge challenges in managing China's economic and social transformation, and it is responding to them by becoming more repressive rather than by opening up. This goes against our instinct that authoritarian regimes need to liberalise to survive, but there is little hard evidence that the Party faces a crisis. The Party has a formidable record of successful adaptation to meet new challenges, which doesn't guarantee it will survive, but makes it rash to assume that it won't. The Nineteenth National Congress in October 2017 confirmed that Xi Jinping is changing the way leadership in China works, and that carries risks. But it's hard to see the restrained triumphalism of the Congress as a sure sign of Party crisis. Perhaps more importantly, we shouldn't assume that China's rise in Asia ends if the Party falls. Is there any reason to believe that a new regime in Beijing would make much difference? Would it be less ambitious, less nationalist or less assertive than the Party, or more willing to accept US predominance in Asia? More likely it would be the opposite.

Third, many people underestimate China's diplomatic weight, because it lacks America's network of alliances and abundant soft power. They assume that China's neighbours are frightened by its growing power and repelled by its high-handed bullying, which draws them to America's side and strengthens its position. All this is true, but it is only half the truth, and not the more important half. It is true that China has no allies, but this may be a strength rather than a weakness, because alliances are often more of a liability than an asset. America must have allies in Asia to remain a strategic power there, because it is not part of the region itself, but it pays a heavy price. The obligation to support and defend Japan, South Korea and other allies imposes military and diplomatic burdens on America which far outweigh the support it gets from them in return. China doesn't have that problem.

Soft power is more clearly a US asset. America remains an attractive country, both as a place to live and as a source of ideas and ideals, even under Donald Trump. No doubt almost everyone in Asia would prefer America to China as a regional hegemon, especially as China starts to use its power more brusquely. But that doesn't necessarily help America much.

Asian countries will only support America against China if they are confident that America will support them, and that it will ultimately prevail. No matter how worried they might be about living under China's shadow, they won't risk China's anger by siding with Washington unless they see a credible US plan for containing China, and clear evidence that the Americans are seriously committed to doing so. They do not see that now, and unless they do they will naturally try to accommodate themselves to China's growing power as best they can.

And of course China has a lot to offer. Even as it grows more slowly, China will still be, over coming decades, by far the biggest source of new economic opportunities for countries throughout Asia. That is epitomised by Beijing's ambitious regional programs, such as the Asian Infrastructure Investment Bank and the Belt and Road Initiative, which demonstrate how Asia's economic future will increasingly centre on China, and how vital good relations with China will be for everyone, whether they like the way China behaves or not. So America faces a much tougher task than many in Washington imagine if they think China's neighbours are eager to alienate Beijing by siding with America.

All this wishful thinking about China's economic, political and diplomatic vulnerabilities makes it impossible for America to respond effectively. But its biggest mistake is to underestimate China as a military power. As we have seen, the nature of power politics puts being willing and able to use armed force at the centre of America's contest with China, and it is easy to assume that this works to America's advantage. Everyone knows that America has the world's biggest defence budget, the world's most advanced technology and vastly greater experience in contemporary combat, and China remains far behind it in all these ways. That's true, and weighs in America's favour, but this too is only half the story. It misses the many factors which weigh against America and in China's favour, in determining the real balance of military advantage. America is a global power with global demands, while China's forces are concentrated in Asia. America must project power over vast distances and operate from a few widely scattered forward bases, while China is close to home, giving it a huge asymmetrical edge. The carriers and other big ships that are the heart of US power-projection into Asia are very vulnerable to China's rapidly growing anti-shipping forces.

The Pentagon has failed to find an effective response to this shift in the balance of military advantage. Back in 2010 it introduced the AirSea Battle concept, which was supposed to explain how America could win a war against China in the Western Pacific by destroying China's anti-shipping capabilities at the start of a conflict with a massive campaign of strikes against bases in China itself. But this made no strategic sense because it would instantly turn any small clash into a major war. This AirSea Battle doctrine was therefore quickly discredited, and nothing has replaced it. So America now appears to have no credible idea of how to use its vast military power to defend its leadership in Asia from China's challenge. That doesn't mean America would lose a conventional war in Asia against China. It means it has no clear way to win it.

Behind the shifting conventional balance looms the even bigger question of nuclear forces. The fact that China is a nuclear power is much more important to the contest than US policy-makers acknowledge. During the Cold War, China's small nuclear arsenal seemed insignificant beside the Soviets' massive capability (and it was aimed primarily at the Soviet Union anyway). After the Cold War, people stopped thinking much about the way nuclear weapons affect relations among major powers, as the focus shifted to fears of proliferation by smaller rogue states like Iraq, Iran and North Korea. As long as everyone assumed that China would happily accept the US-led global order indefinitely, the risk of a nuclear confrontation received little serious attention.

But even after China's emergence as a rival in Asia, most American policy-makers still have largely left China's nuclear forces out of their calculations. At first the working assumption was that China would never allow a confrontation to escalate even to a serious conventional war, because it would be sure to suffer a costly defeat. As this became less tenable, it was assumed instead that China would never allow a conventional war to escalate to a nuclear exchange, because America's far bigger arsenal could do much more damage to China than China's relatively small one could do to America. As one prominent US commentator put it to me not long ago: "The Chinese know that in the end we could leave their country a smoking ruin." That is true, but it misses an important point: America's losses in such a war, though smaller than China's, would still be unimaginably large. China's small nuclear forces could destroy the centres of a dozen major US cities and kill perhaps a million people. If that happened, it would be small consolation to Americans that China had lost a hundred cities and 10 million people.

Of course, neither side is at all likely to start a nuclear war, but that doesn't mean nuclear weapons are not central to their rivalry and the way it plays out. The point about nuclear weapons is not that there is a high likelihood they will be used. It is that even a very remote chance that they might be used imposes big pressures on decision-makers. The mere existence of nuclear arsenals on both sides means that their use can never be ruled out once fighting starts, even at very low levels – because if the conflict escalates, neither side can be sure at what point the other might decide to risk a nuclear strike. Unless they are suicidally reckless, both sides therefore become very cautious about allowing even minor skirmishes. That is why, in the Cold War, Soviet and US forces faced one another toe-to-toe for decades without ever firing a shot.

So far, though, US policy-makers have assumed that America could fight and win a short, sharp conventional war without worrying about nuclear escalation. Hence they seem to have given very little thought to what happens if this assumption turns out to be wrong. We cannot expect the Pentagon to spell out the details of US planning for a nuclear war with China, but we can expect that successive administrations would say enough to show they have understood that China is a serious nuclear adversary, and that they know how to deal with this. There is no evidence of that.

That is because they have not seen China as a serious nuclear power — a nuclear peer — in the way they saw the Soviets in the Cold War, and still see Russia today. Official US policy acknowledges that America and Russia are each equally vulnerable to one another's nuclear forces, and accepts this as the basis of strategic stability between them. Washington has never acknowledged such mutual vulnerability with China. It is hard to see how this makes sense, given that, as we have seen, America is and will remain vulnerable to a Chinese nuclear strike, which, although smaller than a Soviet attack could have been, would still be by far the greatest catastrophe ever to befall the United States.

Why does official American nuclear policy not acknowledge this critical fact? The reason is simple. To do so would embolden Beijing, dismay US allies like Japan, and undermine America's own confidence in its future in Asia. If any armed confrontation with China carries even a slight risk of nuclear war, the threshold for US intervention to support its allies against China is much higher than US policy-makers ever admit, even to themselves. The question "Is this worth even the slightest risk of nuclear war?" will hover over every decision America must make, and most often the answer must be "No."

Of course, the same pressures bear on China. Their leaders too must be very aware of the risk that any confrontation might escalate to a nuclear exchange, so they too have to ask that hard question, and that will make them very cautious about confronting America. But while the risk of nuclear war weighs on both sides, it does not necessarily weigh on them equally. If it is clear to both sides that one of them has less at stake in a crisis than the other, the side with less at stake will be expected to back off first as the crisis escalates. That gives the other side a clear advantage. Such gamesmanship makes all the difference to the power politics of crisis management.

We didn't see this asymmetry at work much in the Cold War, because the two sides were equally committed to preserving their position: neither Washington's nor Moscow's resolve could seriously be doubted. The big exception was the Cuban Missile Crisis, where America prevailed because both sides understood that America had more at stake than the Soviets. That is the same advantage China has in East Asia. Few people, even in Washington, doubt that China cares more about what happens in East Asia than America does, just as no one doubts that America cares more than China about what happens in the Western Hemisphere. So in any East Asian crisis, it is much more likely that America will back off first. Both sides know that, and both sides know that the other side knows it.

In the end, American decision-makers can be less sure that China won't risk a nuclear fight than vice versa. That puts a lot of pressure on America to back off first, and to do so early, and that strengthens China's position. To put it another way, America can only be sure that a confrontation with China won't go nuclear if it is the one that backs off. And the more it believes China understands that, the stronger the incentive to avoid any confrontation at all. We have seen this happening in the South China Sea over the past few years, when it has become clear that America is not willing to risk even a minor naval confrontation with China. And it underlies the president's decision in our Situation Room scenario. The higher the stakes, the more a difference in resolve affects the balance of advantage between strategic rivals, and with nuclear weapons the stakes are very high indeed. This tilts the game in China's favour.

We can see what this means for America's position in Asia if we look at Taiwan. Though it receives less attention than the South China Sea or the East China Sea, this remains arguably the most difficult and dangerous flashpoint in Asia, because US and Chinese interests clash there most intensely and directly. Beijing is unshakably committed not just to preventing any move towards independence for Taiwan, but to progress towards reunification with China. Yet Taiwanese voters are further than ever from agreeing to that. And in Washington it remains an article of faith that America must honour its obligations to Taiwan and prevent Beijing pressing unification by force. American policy-makers argue that failing to support Taiwan would betray a vibrant democracy and fatally undermine America's credibility in Asia.

Back in the 1990s, America certainly had a credible way to defend Taiwan from Chinese attack. America's overwhelming superiority in conventional air and naval forces meant that it could inflict massive losses on China at very little cost. More broadly, America back then could handle the economic consequences of a conflict much more easily than China. But none of that is true now. As we have seen, China today could inflict heavy losses on conventional US forces, and it might well suffer less than America from the war's economic disruption.

Moreover, Beijing would be willing to fight a nuclear war over Taiwan because it is so central to China's national priorities. And the higher this risk becomes, the less likely it is that Washington would come to Taiwan's aid if China attacked, because US intervention would at best produce an indecisive stalemate, and at worst a nuclear war. A crisis over Taiwan would therefore pose in very stark terms the question that hovers over every aspect of America's strategic future in East Asia: is there anything in the region today which is so important to America that it would risk a nuclear war?

This brings us back to the central question of resolve. The biggest mistake US policy-makers have made in dealing with China has been to underestimate how determined it is to replace America as East Asia's leading power. They have taken for granted that America is more committed to maintaining the US-led status quo than China is to overturning it. From Washington, it has been hard to see why Beijing would want to change a regional order which has worked so well for so long – not just for America, but for countries in Asia, including China itself. They don't see that for China the US-led order perpetuates the humiliations inflicted when China's old imperial state and tributary system was destroyed by Western powers in the nineteenth century. They don't see that it perpetuates a subordinate status for China, and stands in the way of it regaining what it sees as its natural place at the head of the regional order. They do not see how important this is, not just to ruling elites in Beijing but also, so far as one can judge, to the vast majority of Chinese. They accept too readily the well-worn assumption that economic growth is all that matters to the Chinese people, and therefore to the Chinese Communist Party. They fail to see, therefore, that the Chinese are just as jealous of their country's standing and reputation, and just as suspicious of others who might seek to degrade it, as Americans are. For the Chinese, and for Xi Jinping, nothing is more important than China regaining its place as a great power, subordinate to no one, and as the primary power in East Asia. That was the key message of the Nineteenth National Congress. Americans would have a truer picture of China's resolve if they understood that China is just as committed to establishing its leadership in East Asia as America is to maintaining its leadership in the Western Hemisphere. This is what makes it such a formidable rival.

Does America have a matching resolve? China is already such an important economic partner that any serious rupture would have almost unthinkable costs for America's economy. And it is already such a formidable strategic adversary that the costs of conflict have become almost unthinkable too. America would have to be very determined indeed to bear these costs and risks, and to convince others that it is willing to do so. To win the contest, America must convince everyone – friends, allies and rivals alike – that despite its distance from Asia, its interests there are so important that it is just as willing to bear those costs as China is.

There is a parallel here with what America did in the Cold War. It met the Soviet challenge by convincing both Moscow and America's allies that it was willing to fight a nuclear war to defend every inch of Western Europe, even though that could mean massive Soviet nuclear attacks on the United States itself. The contest between America and China today is very different from the Cold War, but the essence of America's strategic challenge is much the same: to convince both Beijing and its allies that it is willing to fight a nuclear war and risk massive attacks on American cities, to defend its position in Asia.

How could Washington do that? In the Cold War it was done by leaders explaining to the American people themselves, at length and in detail, that America's survival as a free country depended on containing the Soviets. It was always a hard sell, and no one imagined that America would or should accept the risks of nuclear war for any lesser reason. But generations of American political leaders consistently made the case that the stakes were that high, and generations of Americans voters accepted the argument and supported the commitments that this entailed. This was ultimately what convinced both America's rivals and its partners that America's resolve was real, and its threats and promises were not bluffs. They were persuaded because they could see that Americans themselves believed that America's survival was at stake. Considering the risks of nuclear war involved in the Cold War, it is hard to see how they could have been convinced of US resolve any other way.

If that is right, then America today needs to show its resolve in East Asia in the same way. It must convince Americans that resisting China's challenge in Asia is in their most fundamental national interest — just as essential as containing the Soviet Union was. No American political leader has tried to make that case. Indeed, they hardly ever speak about Asia at all, except in passing and in the most general terms. Neither George W. Bush nor Barack Obama ever gave a major speech on US policy in Asia in the United States itself, and when they spoke about it in Asia they offered boilerplate and bromides, not strategic argument. When more junior figures speak, they recite time-worn claims that US leadership in Asia is essential to protect its economic interests, to support its allies and to ensure America's own security. The closer one looks at these three claims, the less compelling they seem.

There is no reason to assume that America's economic interests in Asia depend on its strategic leadership. American products and investments do not win their place by force of arms — as long as they are competitive, they will find markets and opportunities, just as other countries' do. Europe maintains a massive economic engagement with Asia without playing any strategic role there.

The claim that America must remain in Asia to support its allies makes even less sense, because it confuses means with ends. America's alliances in Asia have been around for so long that they seem part of the furniture, but like all alliances these ones are really just policy tools. They exist to serve fundamental national interests, rather than being ends in themselves. So to say that America must stay in Asia to support its alliances puts the cart before the horse: the alliances are only there to support America's position in Asia. If America doesn't need to maintain that position, then it doesn't need the alliances.

This leaves the central issue of America's own security. If that depended on preventing China from dominating Asia, then the case for continuing US engagement there would be easy to make, whatever the cost. Can this case be made, the way it was in the Cold War? Could China pose the kind of threat to America that the Soviets posed? To answer that, we have to remind ourselves why the Soviet threat was so grave. When the Cold War began, Moscow seemed poised to dominate the entire Eurasian landmass, from the North Atlantic to the North Pacific. It occupied Eastern Europe and was set to seize the rest of Europe as well. It was allied with China, and together they seemed poised to dominate the rest of Asia. Even Japan and India appeared to be at risk of falling under Moscow's sway.

This alarmed Washington because US strategists had always recognised that, surrounded as it is by vast oceans, America's security could only be threatened by a power with uncontested control of all of Eurasia's resources. This possibility had loomed before, in 1917, when Russia collapsed and Germany looked set to win World War I and expand eastwards; and in 1941, when Hitler dominated Europe and aimed to take the Soviet Union and link up with Japan, which looked equally likely to dominate Asia. On each occasion, America chose to intervene. With the advent of the Cold War, the Soviets seemed even better placed to achieve Eurasian hegemony, and this was ultimately why America was willing to carry the immense costs and risks of containing it.

If China may indeed pose this kind of threat, that would be a compelling reason for America to do whatever was necessary to stop it. But it is clear that China's chances of dominating Eurasia as a whole are very remote indeed. It will most likely be the world's richest and strongest state, but it will share the Eurasian landmass with other great powers, including Russia, India and Europe. None of them would be a pushover, and each separately would pose a major challenge to Chinese domination. Together they make it vanishingly improbable. In the decades ahead, China will probably dominate East Asia, but that would not make China strong enough to threaten America in the Western Hemisphere. And if China cannot pose that kind of threat, then it is hard to see how or why Americans would be convinced that they must confront and contain it in Asia. And if that is right, America is very unlikely to accept the burdens required to resist China's bid to become East Asia's dominant power.

It has been clear for a while now, and it should have been clear to Washington, that America faces a stark choice about how to deal with China, and it has only three real options to choose between. It can try to resist and contain China's challenge; it can try to do a deal under which it shares leadership in Asia with China; or it can withdraw. Obama's Pivot was a half-hearted attempt at the first option, which has plainly failed, because he underestimated China's challenge and the commitments that would be required to meet it, and he was not willing to increase his commitments as that became clear. Washington has never seriously considered the second option, though a number of scholars have explored it recently, but now it seems too late to be a real choice. Reaching a power-sharing deal with China would require diplomatic skills which Washington today shows no signs of possessing. Upholding it would require resolve and commitment which, while less than would be needed to maintain primacy, would nonetheless be much greater than America seems able to deliver. And the closer China comes to achieving regional primacy itself, the harder it will become to persuade it to settle for anything less. By default, therefore, America is choosing the third option and gradually withdrawing from Asia. The further this goes, the harder it will be for any president or administration to reverse it and reassert US regional leadership.

To do that, Washington would have to develop a realistic assessment of China's challenge based on convincing judgments of its power and resolve, formulate a comprehensive plan for how America could effectively contain that challenge, make a credible estimate of what that plan would cost, and provide a compelling argument that America's vital interests in Asia justify those costs. It would be hard for any US administration under any president to do all this. But under President Trump it seems simply impossible.

To the extent that Trump can be said to have a policy towards Asia, it is to minimise US commitments there, focus on a narrow trade agenda with Beijing, and tacitly acquiesce to China's assertion of an East Asian sphere of influence. He has no interest in reasserting American leadership of a new global order, as in the mid-1990s. Even if he did, the administration he leads is quite incapable of meeting this challenge. A Truman, an Acheson and a Marshall, with the aid of a Kennan, might have done it. Donald Trump, Rex Tillerson and "Mad Dog" Mattis, with a little help from Jared and Ivana? I don't think so. Under President Trump, the retreat from Asia which began under Obama is probably becoming irreversible.

So we need to prepare ourselves to live in Asia without America.

In early June 2017 Malcolm Turnbull gave the keynote speech at a big defence conference in Singapore. He warned of China's ambition to become the region's leading power, and called on America and its friends and allies in Asia to block this ambition and preserve the old US-led regional order. This was the first time an Australian prime minister had plainly acknowledged the strategic rivalry between China and America, which was long overdue. But Turnbull expressed great confidence that America would prevail over China, and that Asia would therefore continue to flourish under US leadership. So the Australian government is still a long way from acknowledging, to the rest of us or even to itself, what is really happening between America and China, and what it will mean for Australia.

For a long time Canberra's refusal to admit either that a great strategic contest is underway between our major ally and our major trading partner, or that the contest might not go as we'd like, has been symbolised by the bold assertion that "Australia doesn't have to choose between America and China." This has become something of a mantra, intoned by leaders on both sides of politics whenever the question of US–China relations comes up. Malcolm Turnbull even repeated it in his Singapore speech, though he'd made it perfectly clear why it was wrong. It is a perfect example of the very human tendency to confuse a wish with a fact. It is certainly true that Australia doesn't *want* to choose between America and China. Our whole vision of Australia's future assumes that we can avoid such a choice, so that we can keep relying on China to make us rich while America keeps us safe. But in recent years, as the rivalry has escalated, we have more and more faced important choices about when to support America and when to stay on the sidelines. We have not so far been forced to make an all-or-nothing choice to side with one and abandon the other, but that could come if the rivalry escalates further. And if America steps back from Asia, the question of Australia's choices becomes irrelevant. We won't have a choice, because America will no longer be there for us to choose.

But, false or not, the "We don't have to choose" mantra reveals Canberra's assumptions about Australia's future. If we won't have to choose between America and China, it can only be because they are not serious strategic rivals, and if they are not serious strategic rivals, it can only mean that China has decided not to challenge America for regional leadership, because it lacks either the power or the resolve to do so. Canberra, then, is making the same mistake as Washington: it is underestimating China's strength and overestimating America's. That is the story we are telling ourselves to avoid facing what's really happening.

Like so much about Australian policy and politics today, this evasion goes back to John Howard's day. It was he who made an unchallengeable axiom of the idea that there was no tension between Australia's future in Asia and our traditional links with America. He saw this as central to his vision of a relaxed and comfortable country, one that didn't need to worry about its identity or its place in the world. But he realised very well that wasn't true. The harsh reality was brought home to Howard in his first weeks as prime minister, when his instinctively zealous support for America during a crisis over Taiwan earned him a swift kick from Beijing's leaders. They imposed a freeze on relations that lasted for months. Howard got the message: Australia was going to face real choices about how to balance the alliance with America with the economic opportunities offered by China. So he made a deal with Beijing, at a meeting with then-leader Jiang Zemin, late in 1996. Howard told Jiang that Australia's alliance with America was not negotiable, but he promised that nothing Australia would do as a US ally would be directed against China. This was nicely judged, offering neither more nor less than Beijing needed. Jiang was satisfied, and on this basis the relationship with Beijing flourished. It was by far the most effective and consequential diplomatic achievement of Howard's prime ministership, as Howard himself has suggested. But it showed quite plainly that Australia did need to make choices in navigating between Washington and Beijing, and the choice Howard made was a clear sign of the tests to come.

For his part, Howard found it easy to keep his promise to Jiang. While he was prime minister, America's attention was riveted on the Middle East, especially after 9/11. US–China relations recovered swiftly from the Taiwan crisis, and in the years that followed few if any in Washington saw China as a strategic rival. In fact, Howard's understanding with Jiang mirrored Washington's view of the alliance: it too saw no need for Australia to do anything as a US ally directed at China.

That changed on 17 November 2011, when Barack Obama launched his Pivot to Asia with a speech to our parliament in Canberra. His choice of venue was not very subtle. The speech sent a clear message that, for the first time since 1972, America saw China as a rival, and by delivering it in Canberra Obama sent an equally explicit message that America expected Australia's support in responding to this. He knew that this support could not be taken for granted, because Australia's reputation as America's most obliging ally was increasingly counterbalanced by its huge and fast-growing trade with China.

Australia-watchers in Washington had not forgotten that back in 2003 John Howard had welcomed President Hu Jintao to address the parliament on the day before George W. Bush was to do so. It was a powerful symbol of the priority that Canberra, under the famously pro-American Howard, was already giving to relations with Beijing. And since that time, China had overtaken Japan as Australia's biggest trading partner and saved its economy during the global financial crisis. The election of the Chinese-speaking Kevin Rudd appeared, at least at first and from afar, as a further sign of Australia's growing alignment with China, and no one in Washington was too sure where Julia Gillard would take things. So it seemed important in Washington to send a clear message that America expected Australia's support. Obama's simultaneous announcement that US marines would be rotated through Darwin was intended to provide the first tangible evidence of this reinvigorated partnership. It was the first ongoing deployment of US combat forces to Australia since World War II, and it was supposed to show that Australia too was "all in" behind America's plan to deter China in Asia.

But that wasn't the way things turned out. Gillard enthusiastically endorsed the Pivot and welcomed the marines, but it soon became clear that Canberra's support was lukewarm at best. Gillard was determined to appear a good ally to America, but was equally determined to avoid doing serious damage to relations with China. She clearly understood that embracing the Pivot too warmly would violate the understanding with Beijing that had underpinned our flourishing links since 1996. Yet John Howard's deal with Jiang Zemin had suddenly become much harder to honour. America's expectations of Australia had reverted to what they had been before 1972, but back then we cared little about our relations with China. Today we cannot imagine how we could survive a rupture. This is the problem that has haunted Australian foreign policy since November 2011.

Gillard and her successors have responded to this problem in two ways. First, deny there is a problem. Second, give Beijing what it wants, and hope Washington doesn't notice or doesn't mind. The denial was easily done, by simply intoning the "We don't have to choose" mantra. Giving China what it wanted without angering America has been a little more complex. Canberra has had to decide how far it can support America without alienating Beijing, how far we can please China without risking a rebuke from Washington. Our government weighs every decision concerning each country in the light of what it will mean for our relations with the other.

So while we endorsed the Pivot and agreed to host the marines in Darwin, Canberra maintained the fiction that this had nothing to do with China. There was bitter haggling over who would pay for the marines' facilities, a protracted dispute over when and against whom they could operate in a real war, and a marked reluctance in Canberra to consider further big expansions in military cooperation. Washington was astonished when Canberra allowed the contract to run Darwin's port to go to a Chinese company. In May 2015 Tony Abbott showed Canberra's sensitivity to any suggestion that deployments to Darwin were directed at China when he swiftly rebuked a US official who had said that B-1 bombers would be operating from Darwin as part of the US response to Beijing's island-building in the South China Sea. "Our alliance is not aimed at anyone," he said. In the same way, we have joined America in criticising China's conduct in the South China Sea, but have refused to join US freedom of navigation operations there. And while we have grown more receptive to Washington's warnings about the risks of Chinese investment in critical infrastructure, we have not been willing to slow the growth of the broader economic relationship so as to limit our vulnerability to Chinese pressure, as many in Washington would like. After swinging one way and another, we joined China's Asian Infrastructure Investment Bank, ignoring Washington's objections that it would bolster China's strategic weight and influence at America's expense.

The pattern is clear. Under successive governments since 2011, Canberra has offered strong rhetorical support to America's leadership in Asia, but has refused to do anything practical which can unambiguously be seen as directed against China. Our aim throughout has been to convince Washington that we are supporting it against China, and to convince Beijing that we are not. It is, in other words, a policy of systematic duplicity. Some might say that such duplicity is unavoidable and even admirable when one is walking a diplomatic tightrope, but that is only true if the duplicity works. Our problem is that it isn't working: we are fooling no one, except perhaps ourselves.

Certainly the leaders in Beijing are not fooled, but nor are they displeased. They don't expect us to support them against the United States. They just want to us not to support the US against them – to turn us into a neutral. That is a big win for them, because we are America's oldest and closest ally in Asia. They therefore tolerate our lip-service to the alliance so long as we don't give America any tangible or significant support. So far they are getting what they want, so we haven't been punished. Gillard, Abbott and Turnbull have all avoided doing anything that Beijing has seen as violating Howard's understanding with Jiang, and so our relations with China have flourished. Occasionally, however, they give us a flick of the whip to keep us in line, sometimes in private and sometimes in public. Julie Bishop received a famous dressing-down from her Chinese counterpart after she condemned Beijing's declaration of an Air Defense Identification Zone in the East China Sea. In March 2017 Premier Li Keqiang warned Australia not to take sides "in a Cold War fashion" after Bishop gave a speech in Singapore which in some ways prefigured the one Turnbull gave in June. We don't know how Beijing responded to Turnbull's speech, but it would be surprising if it hadn't sounded a stern private warning. The Chinese know how susceptible Australian political leaders are to anything that suggests trouble in the relationship, because our leaders keep reminding them of this. Every time they say, "We don't have to choose between America and China," they remind Beijing how easily a diplomatic frown from China can create an acute political problem for any Australian government by disproving the mantra on which Australian foreign policy is based.

The point has not been lost on Washington. Not long before Obama left office, a senior official vented his frustration to me. "We hate it when your guys keep saying, 'We don't have to choose between America and China'! Dammit, you *do* have to choose, and it is time you chose us!" US policy-makers have clearly been disappointed by our half-hearted support for the Pivot and our reluctance to displease Beijing. They have been worried that Australia is being "Finlandised" – slowly slipping into China's orbit. Washington has mounted a sustained low-key diplomatic effort to counteract this and stiffen Australia's spine. A steady stream of academics, diplomats and senior military officers has been sent out to remind Australians of how much we should fear China, and to encourage us to lean back towards America. It was in Canberra that America's Pacific commander, Admiral Harry Harris, launched his campaign against China's

"Great Wall of Sand" in the South China Sea, and he and others have continually and none-too-subtly urged Canberra to confront China more boldly with freedom of navigation operations of our own there.

Occasionally Washington has shown its displeasure more overtly. In November 2014 President Obama again chose to come to Australia to deliver a major speech about US policy in Asia. The speech became famous for Obama's blunt comments on the Abbott government's climate change policy, but the main thrust of his words concerned China. Just three days before Xi Jinping was to address parliament in Canberra and celebrate the new Australia–China free trade agreement, Obama warned of the risks of getting too close to Beijing. In the most pointedly anti-Chinese speech given by any US president in decades, Obama repudiated the "We don't have to choose" mantra by presenting his view of what our choices are. In scarcely veiled references to the contest with China, he conjured two visions of Asia's future, and then asked:

> Which of these futures will define the Asia Pacific in the century to come? Do we move towards further integration, more justice, more peace? Or do we move towards disorder and conflict? Those are our choices – conflict or cooperation? Oppression or liberty?

There was no mistaking his intention to highlight this choice, and to embarrass Abbott, on the eve of Xi's visit. It was an unusually blunt sign of how, beneath the gushing bonhomie, the relationship has become much chillier in recent years, thanks to Washington's disappointment at our approach to China. But the Obama team mostly refrained from speaking publicly about its dismay. In part that was because they did not want to draw attention to how little their much-puffed Pivot was being supported by America's closest regional ally. In part it was because they feared that more overt demands for Australia to sacrifice its relationship with China might meet with a straight rebuff. But it was also because US policy-makers remained, as we have seen, so ambivalent themselves about the nature and seriousness of China's challenge. They too were eager to believe that no hard choices were needed, because China would be easily dissuaded from its challenge. They too were eager to maintain the US relationship with Beijing, so they too would do nothing that might cause a serious break. Hence the absurd but often-repeated claim that the Pivot was not about containing China, when that is exactly what it was supposed to do.

So Australia got away with half-heartedly supporting the Pivot because Americans themselves were half-hearted about it. And yet we have still expected America to prevail. All this points to the core contradiction in Australia's approach. We want America to defeat the Chinese challenge, and we assume it will, but we have not been prepared to risk our relations with China to help it, because we have assumed that America can manage China without our help. That is despite all the evidence that America can't manage China, with or without our help.

But now Canberra's confidence is slipping. Over the past year or two, Australian policy-makers have become more anxious about China's power and influence, and less confident that America can handle this without clearer and more tangible Australian support. Beijing's flagrant conduct in the South China Sea has at last convinced many of Canberra's optimists that China's challenge to the region's "rules-based order" – by which they mean the US-led status quo – must be taken more seriously. But it has been China's conduct inside Australia that has really got people's attention. Suddenly the Chinese seem to be everywhere. Areas of concern include espionage and cyber-infiltration, the vulnerability of major infrastructure, influence over Australia's Chinese-language press, and surveillance and intimidation of Chinese nationals in Australia, including students. There have been allegations of threats to the academic independence of our universities, of attempts to buy influence over Australian politicians, and of efforts to sway Australian public debate and media coverage about China. Many of these concerns and allegations were brought together in an influential *Four Corners* program in June 2017. These are serious issues which raise important questions about China's influence in Australia and how we manage it, though discussion about them has, perhaps inevitably, been tinged with populist xenophobia. They have nudged both government and Opposition to start raising concerns about China's growing power more frankly than they have been prepared to do before.

At the same time, Donald Trump's presidency has undermined Canberra's confidence both in America's future in Asia, and in Washington's regard for Australia as an ally. Policy-makers were shocked when it became clear after the election that Trump would be as bad a president as everyone had feared, and that his commitment to Asia could not be taken for granted. Even more shocking was the realisation that Trump cared nothing for the alliance. His abusive first phone call with Malcolm Turnbull soon after the inauguration in January overturned Canberra's assumptions about how the two countries communicate, and raised real concerns that, for the first time in living memory, the US president simply didn't care about Australia. Canberra's instinct has been to try to turn this around. This too has nudged the government to start talking more frankly about China than it ever did in Obama's time. It seems that Trump has finally made those in Canberra realise how fragile America's position in Asia is, and so they have now decided to encourage Trump to stand up to China, and to see Australia as a valuable ally in doing this.

This explains Malcolm Turnbull's and Julie Bishop's more forthright remarks in Singapore earlier this year. It also explains the strange and sad spectacle of the Australian government trying to pretend that Donald Trump is anything like a normal president leading a competent administration. Most significantly, it may explain Turnbull's extraordinary decision to offer Donald Trump unqualified support in his threats to launch a war against North Korea. Such a war would probably and quickly become the worst the world has seen in many decades, and Donald Trump is the last person in the world to be trusted with a blank cheque on such a matter. The costs to Australia of encouraging Trump to launch such a war, and of joining in ourselves, could be immense.

The Turnbull commitment was made in a few lines during a radio interview. From what he said, there is no evidence that he or his government had given the matter any serious thought. In his very brief statements since then, the prime minister has said nothing about the circumstances under which such a war could be justified, and nothing to explain why taking part in it would serve Australia's interests, beyond the fact that we are America's ally. Never before in our history has a government so blithely committed Australia to such a momentous strategic action with so little thought or explanation. It is not clear why Turnbull did it, but the most likely reason was to bolster Trump's regard for Australia as an ally, as Turnbull and his colleagues become more and more worried about China. One wonders if it worked: knowing Trump, probably not.

*

So what now? Around the time this essay is published, the government plans to release its new foreign policy white paper. China and America will inevitably be the focus. It will have to say something about how the government sees China as a partner and as a regional power, and how it sees America's future as Asia's leading power and Australia's essential ally. It is not hard to guess some of what it will say. It will acknowledge how far and fast China's wealth and power have grown, how much Australia has benefited from our relationship with China so far, and how much more we stand to gain in the future. It will acknowledge concerns about how China might use its power both in the region and to pressure Australia. It will say that Australia wants to see a rules-based order in Asia which will constrain China's power by upholding the rule of international law, which has done so much to keep Asia stable and prosperous for so long. It will declare that strong American engagement in the region is essential to maintaining the rules-based order. It will speak of the need to integrate China into that order so that it is a positive rather than a negative factor in the regional system. All of this is very predictable. But then comes the test.

Will the white paper declare the government's perfect confidence that America will continue to be the primary power? Or will it acknowledge real doubts about America's future in Asia? Will it acknowledge that Canberra's vision of regional order based on US power is directly contrary to China's ambition to build a new order centred on Beijing? Will it explain how China can be persuaded to abandon this ambition, and if it cannot be persuaded, whether it can be compelled? If not, will it explore how Australia will manage its relationship with China and avoid being subject to China's power if America is not there to uphold the rules and norms that we hope will protect us? In other words, will the foreign policy white paper, despite everything that has happened since 2011, still cling to the idea that America will remain the dominant power in Asia, and that China will happily accept this?

If it does do this, then the government, and Australia, will have failed once again to come to terms with the profound shifts that are transforming our international setting, and will once again have lost the chance to start responding to them effectively and realistically. It will be a triumph for wishful thinking over serious policy, and a further confirmation of the systemic failure in political and policy leadership that has afflicted Australia for at least a decade, and arguably since the turn of the century.

Of all our recent political leaders, Turnbull did at one time go furthest beyond wishful thinking and seriously discuss these questions, but that was before he became prime minister. Labor in Opposition has ventured a little further than the government. Penny Wong, as shadow foreign minister, has spoken quite seriously about our relations with China, but her words suggest that she too assumes that we will face no hard choices, and that America will always be there in Asia for us.

It is perhaps understandable that none of our leaders wants to break the bad news, especially when the implications of that news are so unwelcome and unsettling. Some of them perhaps genuinely believe, in the face of all the evidence, that America will remain the leading power in Asia with Beijing's acquiescence. Many others, and many of those who advise them, understand that this is not so, but believe there is no point admitting the truth because there is nothing we can do about it anyway. They say, or imply, that acknowledging the way America is losing ground to China might only speed things up by undermining America's position and emboldening China, so best to pretend it is not happening. This quiescent approach follows quite naturally from the view — common until recently among more thoughtful people in Canberra — that we need do nothing about it because America and China could be relied upon to drift gradually and automatically towards a stable new relationship which both satisfied China's ambitions and preserved US influence. The habit of quiescence is hard to break now that this happy outcome looks less and less likely. So Canberra has succumbed to a tacit fatalism about Australia's future in Asia. This carries dangers. An obvious one is that we fail to prepare to operate in the very different Asia. A less obvious one is that we unthinkingly assume that, if all else fails, we would and should go to war with America against China, rather than see China take America's place. That is happening in Canberra now.

In one way it makes a kind of sense. If it is true, as both government and Opposition tell us, that Australia can only be secure and prosperous while America remains the leading power in Asia, then it follows that we should be willing to do whatever it takes to ensure that it does remain the leading power. And if it is true, as I have argued in this essay, that to remain the leading power, America must convince China that it is willing to fight a major war to do so, and that it can only do that if it really is willing to fight that war, then it follows that Australia too must be willing to fight China by America's side. The stern logic of power politics applies to us as much as to the Americans. We cannot expect them to prevail in Asia if they are not willing to fight, and we cannot expect them to be willing to fight if we are not.

So it is in some ways unsurprising that over the past few years the prospect of such a war has become the principal focus of our defence policy. This is clear from recent defence white papers, especially the last one, published in 2016. Its unmistakable underlying message was that Australia's strategic priority is now to support America in defending the rules-based regional order from China, and this is what the ADF is being prepared to do. That is a major shift from the old emphasis on defence self-reliance, which gave priority to independent operations for defending Australian territory. In fact, the word "self-reliance," which peppered every defence policy statement since 1976, virtually disappeared from the last white paper. Instead it took us back to the old "forward defence" idea of the 1950s and 1960s, when we built forces to support our allies in their wars against rival powers in Asia. The return to this approach is clear in decisions to invest heavily in high-end air and naval forces designed to combine with American forces in major conflicts, including new frigates, and the replacement of the Collins submarines with bigger boats designed to operate alongside the US Navy in the South China Sea and beyond. It is very strange that this momentous shift in national policy has occurred without any serious debate.

It might seem absurd that ministers who baulk at a freedom of navigation operation in the South China Sea are nonetheless willing to contemplate joining a major war there, but it fits the pattern of thoughtless tough talk on national security which has become so central to our politics since 2001. Turnbull's eager promise to support Trump over North Korea showed how far this has now gone, and confirms the government's breezy eagerness to talk up our willingness to go to war without thinking about what that might involve.

Malcolm Turnbull didn't always think this way. Back in 2011 he criticised the 2009 defence white paper's premise "that we should base our defence planning and procurement on the contingency of a naval war with China in the South China Sea." But that is just what he is now doing.

Still, one wonders how the conversation would run in Canberra if our Situation Room scenario played out differently, and Malcolm Turnbull got a call from the president asking Australia to send forces to join an escalating war with China in the South China Sea, say, or over Taiwan. No one talks about this much in Canberra, but it is a very important question. The consensus is that he, or any other prime minister, would almost certainly say yes, "simply because he would have no choice."

I think that is quite wrong. The prime minister would certainly have a choice, although it would not be an easy one. Saying no would weaken, and perhaps destroy, the alliance on which we depend. Saying yes would plunge Australia into what might easily be the biggest war since 1945.

One hopes that if ever the decision must be faced and taken, it would be based on realistic ideas of what was involved. If it was, I think the answer would almost certainly be no. It is possible to imagine circumstances in which it would, even so, be right to go to war, as it was right to go to war in 1939. But whether it would be right in the circumstances of a US–China clash in Asia over Taiwan, say, is very far from clear. And it is absolutely clear that Australia's decision should not be delegated to Donald Trump of all people.

Of course, no one in Canberra wants or expects a war with China. The muddled thinking behind our posturing is that it will help deter China in its push for regional leadership and leave the region as we'd like it to be, in peace and under US leadership. But the thought that if all else fails, America's primacy could and would be preserved by armed force nonetheless does a lot to underpin our leaders' confidence that, come what may, we will never find ourselves living in an Asia dominated by China. This is a big mistake because, as we have seen, America has no real reason to fight China for primacy in Asia, shows little real interest in doing so and has no chance of succeeding if it tries. Until our leaders realise that, they will not address the reality that we are, most probably, soon going to find ourselves in an Asia dominated by China, where America plays little or no strategic role at all.

Australia is going to have a more independent foreign policy in the new Asia – more independent of Washington, that is – whether it likes it or not. Many people welcome this, because they think depending less on America is a sign of greater national maturity. But that is itself, I think, a little immature. There is nothing inherently wrong with depending on others, as long as it works. Depending on America to keep Asia stable and Australia secure has worked very well for Australia for a long time. The benefits of dependence have far outweighed the costs. If America could remain the uncontested dominant power in Asia in future, there would be no good reason to step away from it. But that is not going to happen. In fact, the question of whether we should seek more independence by stepping away from America is irrelevant, because America is stepping away from Asia, and that means it is stepping away from us. Independence is not an appealing option to choose, but an unavoidable and uncomfortable fact to be managed. We are going to be on our own.

But won't America still be there to support Australia even if it pulls back from Asia? Many people think it would, because of the way we talk of the alliance as based on enduring bonds of history, culture and values, rather than just as a convenient, useful alignment of strategic interests. This image of the alliance as rooted in our identity is reflected in the way Turnbull spoke of it when announcing his commitment to support Donald Trump on North Korea. He spoke of Australia and America standing "shoulder to shoulder" and being "joined at the hip."

Alas, international relations don't work that way. There are no examples of alliances – real alliances involving real commitments and costs, which are the only kind that matter – surviving on sentiment alone, without clear shared interests and objectives. Our interests and objectives in Asia have aligned closely with America's in recent decades, but that won't last as America's strategic engagement in Asia dwindles. We have seen this happen before. Our alliance with Britain evaporated overnight when it withdrew strategically from Asia in the early 1970s, despite our even closer links of history, language and values. Ministerial speeches larded with sentimental clichés won't preserve the alliance once the practical strategic purpose is past.

Policy-makers are reluctant to face this because they have convinced themselves that Australia simply cannot survive without the alliance. They often say, for example, that it is essential to our defence, because the need to fight alongside one another seamlessly means our forces are inseparably intertwined with those of the US. It is certainly true that our forces are much more intertwined today than they were in the 1980s and 1990s, because we have chosen to develop them for coalition rather than independent operations. And it is true, of course, that we would have to spend a lot more on defence if we cannot depend on America as we have done for so long. But it is not true that we have no alternatives. We just haven't thought much about them recently.

The same is true of diplomacy. For a long time our primary diplomatic objective in Asia has been to bolster support for the US-led order. In future we need to focus on how best to protect our interests in a very different order, reflecting the new realities of power and influence. So it is important that we understand something of how that new Asian order will emerge, and how it will work.

*

Japan is the key to East Asia's emerging order as China's power grows and America's wanes. Japan's alliance with America has been the keystone of America's strategic position in Asia. While the alliance lasts America will remain a major regional power, and when it ends America's role in Asia will end with it. So we can best understand how America's position in Asia might collapse by considering the future of the alliance. Outwardly the alliance looks robust, because it has served the interests of each side so well for so long, but the shift in wealth and power towards China changes the calculations for both America and Japan. For America, the costs of the alliance are growing, while the benefits are not. China's rise makes it both a more valuable economic partner and a more formidable military adversary, and so the costs to America of protecting Japan against China go up both economically and strategically. (As we have seen, the same is true on a different scale of North Korea, once its ICBMs can target American cities.)

By the same token, the benefits of the alliance to Japan are falling, as US support in a crisis becomes less certain. This worries Japan more and more as both China and North Korea look more and more threatening. There will come a point when Tokyo reluctantly concludes that America simply cannot be relied upon any longer. That might happen quite quickly if a mishandled crisis suddenly reveals a collapse in US credibility. Donald Trump's presidency makes that more likely. The key question for Japan would then be whether to build its own nuclear weapons. There is a very real chance it would – especially if South Korea had already done so, as it easily might. Then there would be no compelling reason for either side to preserve the US–Japan alliance, and it would swiftly collapse, and with it the US position in Asia. This is a very real possibility.

What would Japan do then? Many people hope that it would re-emerge as a great power, leading a coalition of like-minded countries, including Australia, to balance China's power and prevent it from dominating the region. This seems to be what Japan's current prime minister, Shinzo Abe, has in mind. Tony Abbott was a fan of the idea, which explains his enthusiasm for building an alliance with Japan, symbolised by his impulsive and ill-fated desire to buy Japanese submarines. But it is hard to see this working, because Japan would find it hard to unite countries against China. They all value their own links with China, which they would be reluctant to sacrifice at Japan's direction and to serve Japan's interests unless China started looking much more threatening than it does today.

So it is much more likely that Japan would take a more modest course, accepting China's regional primacy but ensuring that it can resist Chinese pressure on really vital issues by maintaining strong air and naval forces, backed by a minimum nuclear deterrent. This would be Japan as a middle power. If Japan takes this path, China would find it relatively easy to convince the rest of East Asia to accept its leadership, because the region's other countries lack the weight, individually or even together, to balance China's power.

Beyond East Asia and the Western Pacific, China faces much bigger challenges, especially from India. India is a great power of immense potential, and though it will probably remain weaker than China for a long time to come, it certainly has the power to impose some limits on Beijing's expanding influence. But it is not clear how that will work and what it will mean. One view is that China and India will become rivals over an entire region stretching from the western Indian Ocean to the Western Pacific – the so-called Indo-Pacific region. Many people in Canberra share this view. If India reaches anything like its potential, the two powers will be evenly enough matched to ensure that neither could win this contest, so neither would dominate the whole Indo-Pacific. Instead there would be an unstable and contested balance of power that would be very uncomfortable to live with.

But there are other possibilities. India cannot hope to dominate the Western Pacific the way China can, and China cannot hope to dominate the Indian Ocean the way India can, so why should either try? They could agree to stay out of one another's backyards, which would make more sense than competing for a bigger prize that neither has any chance of winning. If this happens, we would see two separate spheres of influence, with China dominating East Asia and the Western Pacific, and India dominating South Asia and the Indian Ocean. The boundary between them follows the line that separates the two oceans and regions through Southeast Asia and into the South Pacific. Australia sits on that boundary, which would give us important diplomatic and strategic opportunities in the new Asia.

So does much of Southeast Asia. Many people think that the countries of Southeast Asia, united in the Association of Southeast Asian Nations (ASEAN), will play a key role in shielding Australia from China by balancing and limiting its power. That is too optimistic. ASEAN has loomed so large in Asia for so long that it is tempting to see it as a kind of great power in its own right and a potential counterweight to China. But that is not how ASEAN works. Its strength has always been managing relations among members, not managing their collective relations with others. That has hardly mattered, because Asia has been free of great-power rivalry almost since ASEAN was founded. Now, for the first time, the vision of a regional order based on "the ASEAN Way" is meeting the realities of great-power politics, and ASEAN can't cope. Its members are too diverse – historically, geographically, economically – to act together as a single player in the contest over Asia's future. Vietnam's interests when it comes to China are very different from Indonesia's, Laos's interests are very different from the Philippines', and Singapore's very different from Myanmar's. None of them wants to live under China's shadow, but each of them has vital interests in its relations with Beijing, and none is willing to sacrifice its interests for others'. That makes it easy for China to divide them, as we have seen it do already over the South China Sea. If Beijing plays its cards well, it can ensure the members of ASEAN won't work together to balance and limit China's power.

That doesn't mean Southeast Asia won't matter. Countries such as Vietnam and Indonesia will be significant regional powers in their own right. But they will not be strong enough to counterbalance China's power or prevent it dominating East Asia, and they will be determined to keep relations with Beijing at least workable. Their aim will be to maximise their freedom to manoeuvre and their independence of China's influence, and we can expect them to show a lot of flexibility and a bit of guile in doing that.

All this has big implications for Australia's diplomacy. China will obviously become our most important and demanding interlocutor, but relationships with others will be key to managing Beijing's demands as painlessly as possible. Of the great powers, India will be the most important to us, because it will want to limit China's influence in the Indian

Never again miss an issue. Subscribe and save.

☐ **1 year auto-renewing print and digital subscription** (4 issues) $69.95 incl. GST (save 24%). Subscriptions outside Australia $109.95.

☐ **1 year print and digital subscription** (4 issues) $79.95 incl. GST (save 13%). Subscriptions outside Australia $119.95.

☐ **2 year print and digital subscription** (8 issues) $149.95 incl. GST (save 18%).

☐ Tick here to commence subscription with the current issue.

All prices include postage and handling.

PAYMENT DETAILS I enclose a cheque/money order made out to Schwartz Publishing Pty Ltd. Or please debit my credit card (MasterCard, Visa or Amex accepted).

CARD NO. ☐☐☐☐ ☐☐☐☐ ☐☐☐☐ ☐☐☐☐ ☐☐☐☐

EXPIRY DATE _____ / _____ CCV _____ AMOUNT $ _____

CARDHOLDER'S NAME _____

SIGNATURE _____

NAME _____

ADDRESS _____

EMAIL _____ PHONE _____

Freecall: 1800 077 514 **or** +61 3 9486 0288 **email:** subscribe@quarterlyessay.com **quarterlyessay.com**
Digital-only subscriptions are available from our website: quarterlyessay.com.au/subscribe

Quarterly Essay
REPLY PAID 90094
CARLTON VIC 3053

Ocean region, which should mean it has a long-term interest in limiting China's sway over Australia. We should be able to use this to our advantage with adroit diplomacy, using India's concerns to deflect Chinese pressure and vice versa – a version of the classic buffer-state diplomacy. Exploiting our position between China and India in this way will require a whole new set of diplomatic skills. Japan would be a less valuable partner for us if it settles for a middle-power role, because it will have little interest in supporting Australia.

Southeast Asia will become more important to us, regaining the central place it had in the 1950s and 1960s, when much of Asia's great-power politics played out there. Since then, and especially since the mid-1990s, our interest in and engagement with Southeast Asia has waned. We will need to do a lot more there. That doesn't necessarily mean we should try to join ASEAN, because ASEAN itself won't have much influence on the issues that matter most to us. Nor will grand gestures like the planned ASEAN–Australia Summit in Canberra in 2018 do much. We should focus on deepening our relationships with the most important and effective Southeast Asian powers, especially Vietnam, Thailand, Singapore and Indonesia. We should not expect to build a "united front" with these countries, because our situations and interests are too different. They will not always be on our side against China, nor will we always be on theirs. But there will be important opportunities for us to cooperate with them on specific issues where our interests align in deflecting China's power, and we'd be wise to start building the foundations for such cooperation as soon as possible. That will not always be easy. The power balance between us and our Southeast Asian neighbours is shifting their way fast, as their economies outstrip ours, and after decades of liberalisation the political trends in many of them are heading the other way, so our perspectives may often diverge.

Indonesia presents special challenges. It is the biggest and wealthiest Southeast Asian power, and also the closest to us. It has huge potential: by 2030 it is projected to have the fifth-biggest economy in the world, three and a half times larger than Australia's. Whether it realises that potential, and how it uses its power if it does, remains a mystery, but Australia cannot afford to assume it won't become a very powerful country indeed, second only to China in shaping our geopolitical environment. Geography alone means that Indonesia would be a vital potential ally if China became aggressively hostile. By the same token, it is also, of course, a potentially serious adversary. Ensuring that Indonesia is a strategic asset rather than a liability in the new Asia will be among our highest national priorities. It will require a big shift from the fragile and narrowly transactional relationship we have today, and this will be complicated by worrying political trends there: the erosion of democratic reforms, and the slide towards authoritarianism and away from secularism.

Finally, where does America fit? We are so used to thinking of it as a major ally that it is hard to imagine any other kind of relationship. But America will be an important country to us even if it no longer guarantees our security. It will remain a very powerful state and a vibrant society with a huge amount to offer – in trade and investment, culture, education and technology, including military technology. It won't be the dominant power in Asia, but it will have both the means and the motive to exert some influence over China's conduct – including in East Asia – through the global system in which it will play a key role. That could help us, so we should do what we can to build a new relationship with America – a post-alliance relationship – which maximises our opportunities. Forty years ago we managed the transition to a post-alliance relationship with Britain quite well, and doing the same with America will be an important task in the years ahead.

LIVING WITH CHINA'S POWER

We are plunging into the unknown here, facing a future in East Asia that is dominated by China rather than America. China will exercise more influence over Australia than any country has ever done before, except Britain and America. Sometimes in a class I ask students how they feel about this. Mostly they are young people – undergrads, graduate students or early-career public servants. I give them four options. Would it be "really bad," "not great," "okay," or "quite good"? Almost none say, "quite good." Only a small minority say, "really bad." Most say, "okay" or "not great": they don't want it, but they are not appalled by it and are willing to give it a go. That suggests they find the idea less frightening than their elders, certainly than those who discuss policy in Canberra's inner circles. When I ask older people the same question, a lot more answer, "really bad." What strikes me, however, is how little most of us have thought about how we could deal with it. That is not perhaps surprising, because for so long we have been encouraged to assume that it will never happen, and it is hard to imagine a world so different from what we have known. But now that it is clear how quickly and profoundly Asia is changing, it is time to think more clearly about what it would mean. We don't want to underestimate the risks and challenges, because they will be real and serious, but we don't want to exaggerate them either. If it is going to happen, and it seems there is no realistic way we can stop it, then we must learn to live with it and make the best of it.

Some will say it smacks of appeasement even to talk about how we should learn to live with China's power, when instead we should just be resisting it. That is easy to say if we can comfortably assume that China's rise to regional primacy can be easily and cheaply stopped. But if, as this essay argues, that is not so, then those who speak of appeasement have to say what kind of costs and risks they think we should be willing to bear to stop it. Power politics in Asia today suggests that China would need to be confronted with the risk of a major war to be deterred.

As we have seen, this idea of war has a certain shadowy standing in Canberra, but mostly among those who are sure it will never come to that, because they are sure China will soon back off in the face of US power and resolve. The less credible this becomes, the more directly those who decry appeasement must confront the real alternative: is the prospect of an Asia dominated by China bad enough to be worth fighting a major war over? Leaving to one side the practical question of whether enough countries with sufficient power would share our views and join the struggle, the answer depends on what is really at stake. Again, talk of appeasement suggests that the stakes today are comparable to the stakes in 1938, when it was no exaggeration to say that the future of liberal democracy, indeed of civilisation, was at stake. People sometimes speak today in similar terms about China's rise. They say that China's growing power and influence poses a direct threat to our liberal-democratic political system and the values that underpin it, and that our system and values cannot survive unless China's power is curbed.

Plainly China's values – or the values of China's rulers – are different from ours, and there is much that happens there that we find disturbing or worse. We would, I think, pay a very high price to prevent those values and the political system that reflects them being imposed on Australia. Whether we'd pay the price of a major war is a question we might hope never to have to face. But we do not face that question yet. The question we should consider now, more carefully than we have so far felt the need to do, is what kind of threat China as the dominant power in East Asia would, or does, pose to the fundamental values on which our society is based, and the institutions that support them. How seriously are our values threatened simply by the fact that China's political system is based on different ones? And how serious is the risk that China's values and system might be imposed on us in Australia?

Answering these questions will require us to think about values rather differently from the way they mostly figure in our talk about foreign affairs. That talk often presumes that values sit on one side of the argument and interests on the other. That is sometimes true, but only when the stakes are relatively low. When the stakes are high, the choices we face are not between interests and values, but between competing values on both sides of the argument. In Asia today, as so often in international relations, the big choice we face is between justice on one side and peace on the other, and peace weighs heavily when the alternative is major war.

We don't know much about how China plans to use its power in East Asia. Its leaders say nothing about this beyond the blandest platitudes, and they probably have no clear idea themselves. What we fear, and what those who condemn accommodation as appeasement assume, is that they plan to impose a harsh and oppressive hegemony which would force fundamental changes to Australia's political system, social order and economic prospects. That is not impossible. Beijing could one day try to impose its brand of authoritarian politics, dictate national policies and control our economy to its advantage. At the worst it could invade the country and subject it to direct rule from Beijing. These are the kinds of things that hegemonic powers have done throughout history, including in the recent history of the twentieth century, which is so vivid to us. They are what Nazi Germany, Imperial Japan and the Soviet Union sought to do with their power.

Perhaps some people in China have ambitions like this already, and such ideas might become more widespread as China's power grows. But there is no evidence that this is how China's leaders see things today. Their territorial ambitions seem limited to the lands that China already occupies or claims, including of course Taiwan. They show no desire to proselytise an ideology or export a political system. Nor do they want radical change in the regional or global economic order which has served China so well. They do want to reshape the economic order to serve China's economy as it grows and changes. They want to protect their own ideology and political system from outside influence, and to guarantee their own territorial security. And they want to reassert China's status as a great power, and as the leading power in East Asia. This is all ambitious enough, but it means they have no need to impose a harsh hegemony on their neighbours. It also seems that China's leaders have studied enough history to know that even the strongest states should husband their power. Countries that waste power by throwing their weight around more than is necessary soon come to grief. That suggests that they will seek no more influence in East Asia, and over Australia, than they need to achieve their key objectives.

Beijing's efforts will naturally focus on issues that touch directly on China's interests. The first priority will be anything that relates to China's internal affairs, and especially the role of the Communist Party. We can expect more and more pressure on us not to do anything that Beijing sees as interfering in China's internal affairs or undermining the authority or legitimacy of the Party. The second priority will be to influence us on anything that affects China's position in East Asia. China will pressure us to accept, if not welcome, its rise to regional leadership, and like all preponderant powers it will be jealous of its place and eager to deter any support for a rival; should one appear, our attitude towards it will be closely monitored. If we do end up on the boundary between China's and India's spheres of influence, then China will be particularly concerned to make sure we don't swing too much India's way – and vice versa. And third, it will always be willing to apply pressure for economic advantage.

If this is the kind of leadership it seeks, Beijing will be following America's example in the Western Hemisphere. Under the Monroe Doctrine, Washington has exercised effective leadership and protected its key interests throughout North and South America at little cost to itself and mostly without intruding too much on the affairs of its neighbours. This seems to be how China aims to wield its power in East Asia. Yet it is not clear that an authoritarian country like China can be as tolerant a hegemon as the United States, and even if it is, this version of Chinese leadership, so modest compared to others in recent history, would mean much greater intrusion into Australia's affairs than we have ever experienced or contemplated by any country other than Britain or America. In his Singapore speech, Malcolm Turnbull likened China's regional ambitions to "a latter-day Monroe Doctrine in this hemisphere" and, as we have seen, made it clear that this would be unacceptable to Australia. But unless we can come up with better ideas of how to prevent it than Turnbull had to offer, we are going to have to live with it. So we have to think a bit more about what it would mean, and how to manage it.

To start with, it is worth remembering that the situation we now face is new to us, but not to others. Most countries throughout history have lived in the shadow of great powers and been subject to their influence much more than they would wish. We have been lucky, because the countries that have had the most influence over us have also been the ones we have felt closest to, and whose interests and values have aligned most naturally with ours. We have mostly assumed that they would not use their power at our expense, and that has largely been true. Other countries have not had that luxury, and now we do not either. For us, it's welcome to the real world, as we come out from under America's wing.

We can get a clearer idea of what this will mean by looking at other countries' experience of the way great powers exert influence over weaker ones. It is not as straightforward as we often assume, because even relatively weak sovereign states have a formidable capacity to control what happens in their territory. Great powers cannot simply dictate to smaller ones unless they intervene with armed force. Short of that, they exercise influence by offering rewards or, more often, by imposing costs. In fact, a key measure of a state's power is its ability to impose costs on other states at low cost to itself. China's power over Australia will be reflected in its ability to impose costs on us to persuade us to do what it wants, and the stronger it becomes, the greater the costs it will be able to impose. This means, however, that weaker states have choices about how they respond to pressure. Even a very weak state can defy a great power if it is willing to pay the price. North Korea has shown this over many years: it has been able to defy US pressure to abandon its nuclear program because it has been willing to accept the costs that America has imposed.

Likewise, we will be able to defy China's pressure if we choose, but China will be able to inflict heavy costs on us if we do. It will not be able to dictate to us, but it will be able to shape our choices very powerfully. This is already happening, of course. It is often said that "China does not have a veto over our foreign policy," and that's true. Australia could, if it wished, do lots of things that China would bitterly oppose, like open diplomatic relations with Taiwan, advocate independence for Tibet or campaign for the overthrow of the Chinese Communist Party. But Beijing could exact a very high price for doing any of these, so we choose not to. As China's power in Asia grows, its capacity to impose costs on us will grow, and that will give it greater and greater influence over our choices. That's the reality of power. So our task, as we learn to live with China's power, is to learn how to make those choices well, so that we can preserve maximum independence over our most important issues at minimum cost. From now on, that is what our foreign policy will be all about.

Where can this kind of pressure be applied? The most obvious point is the economic relationship. China finds this easy, because it is already such an important partner for so many countries, and it offers such rich opportunities in the future. Sometimes it threatens markets directly. In recent years it has cut tourism to South Korea after it allowed America to base missile defence units there, banned Norwegian salmon after a Chinese dissident was awarded the Nobel Peace Prize, and limited Mongolian mineral imports after the Dalai Lama visited. But more often it applies economic pressure indirectly by threatening future opportunities, either explicitly or implicitly. It did this to John Howard back in 1996, and to British prime minister David Cameron when he met the Dalai Lama in 2012.

If this hasn't happened more to Australia recently, it is because we have been so careful not to offend. It is Canberra's choice not to hold official meetings with the Dalai Lama which would irritate Beijing, but such choices are influenced by the price we would pay if such meetings occurred. Sometimes we may get these calculations wrong by exaggerating the costs we would pay for displeasing Beijing, and it may sometimes pay to be a little more thick-skinned. Managing such pressure in the future will require a cooler head and steadier nerve than we have ever shown in the past.

It will be harder to respond to the more insidious forms of Chinese pressure and influence that have recently become worrying, such as control over critical infrastructure, attempts to influence media coverage and public opinion, buying influence with political donations, surveillance and harassment of Chinese students studying here, and trying to influence what gets taught at our universities. These all remind us, if we needed reminding, that China will use whatever means come to hand to achieve its objectives, just as other countries do, and neither its objectives nor its means will necessarily be benign. It is no good hoping that Beijing will stop doing these things if we ask nicely. If we don't want to live with them, we will need to take steps ourselves to curtail them, and pay the costs accordingly. Some things are easy, like banning foreign political donations. Others are more difficult: it is hard to see how we can prevent China using its money to promote favourable media coverage without curtailing the freedom of the press. Nor would it be easy to ban political donations from Australians who support China's positions. We can certainly resist Chinese pressure over what gets taught in our universities, but we'll have to live with the consequences if China responds by telling its students not to come here.

Beyond these overt and insidious forms of Chinese influence lies the spectre of strategic pressure – applied through armed force. It can range all the way from direct attack to subtle and indirectly threatening gestures which nonetheless raise in our minds the possibility of force being used. A direct Chinese attack on Australia remains very unlikely, even if our alliance with America fails, if only because our geography makes us a difficult target – unless we pose, or support America in posing, direct threats to China. But China will increasingly use its military to display its power, even without threatening our continent itself. Over the past few years Chinese naval taskforces have started to operate close to northern Australia in classic displays of strategic reach. In the future Beijing could ramp up pressure by contesting Australia's title to remote bits of Australian territory, like our Antarctic islands, or by starting to build closer defence links with and even deploying forces to our small South Pacific neighbours. That would get Australia's attention. Along with so much else, strategic pressure from China is something we will have to learn to live with, and it will influence the way we think about our own armed forces.

No amount of armed force will ever allow us to impose our will on China, but a well-designed force could prevent China from imposing its will on us by raising the costs and risks to China of attacking us high enough to persuade it to give up. This is how middle powers have always dealt with more powerful adversaries, and it sometimes works. It could work for us because Australia has a lot of geographical advantages – it is an island, it is big and it is remote. But we can no longer afford to assume that America would come to our aid, nor can we presume on the support of our neighbours. The only forces we can rely on will therefore be our own.

In the past, under the rubric of self-reliance, we have planned to defend the continent independently from the kind of weak forces that Indonesia has maintained, but we have never seriously considered trying to defend the continent independently from a major Asian power. It is not impossible, but it would be difficult, and expensive. We would have to organise our armed forces very differently, and spend a lot more on them – perhaps twice as much as we do today. We would have to focus our efforts on the most critical operational tasks. Our geography dictates that the key to our defence, and the defence of our neighbours, is to prevent an adversary projecting power by sea or air over the oceans that surround us, so we'd need to build a force focused on that task. That would look very different from the military we are building and planning today.

Then there is the question of nuclear weapons. Australia considered acquiring nuclear weapons back in the 1950s and 1960s, but abandoned the idea when strategic circumstances changed in the late 1960s and early 1970s. Nuclear forces made no sense at all while Asia remained stable and

America's strategic commitment to Asia was assured. But as America's power and commitment in Asia fades, this has big implications for the nuclear choices of America's Northeast Asian allies, as we have seen. It is now quite likely that, despite the immense cost and difficulty involved, both Japan and South Korea will become nuclear powers within a couple of decades. And the logic that drives them has implications for others. Though not a near prospect, the chance of Indonesia or Vietnam considering nuclear weapons later in the century is higher now than it was when US primacy seemed unchallengeable.

Australia today faces no urgent choices, because it faces far less direct threats than Japan and South Korea, but the trends which undermine their confidence in America's nuclear guarantees affect us too. No matter how capable our conventional forces were, an adversary could force concessions or capitulation by threatening a nuclear strike, to which an Australia without its own nuclear forces would have no response. The chilling logic of strategy therefore suggests that only a nuclear force of our own, able credibly to threaten an adversary with massive damage, would ensure that we could deter such a threat ourselves. This would only require a small force, but it would need to have very long-range, high-yield warheads and be very secure from preemptive strike. It might look something like Britain's submarine-based nuclear force.

Let me be quite clear. I am neither predicting nor advocating that Australia should acquire nuclear weapons. On the contrary, I find the idea appalling. But the fundamental changes in our strategic circumstances since the early 1970s mean that the consequences for us of not having nuclear weapons might well be very different in the future than they have been in decades past, and it is untenable to think that this won't mean the question will have to be re-examined.

It may well be that as US power fades and the new regional order emerges, it will become clear that only countries with their own minimum nuclear deterrent will have the capacity to stand up to a great power independently. That capacity has always been the hallmark of a middle power. If so, Australia's choice about nuclear weapons would be a choice between being a middle power and a small power. If China, or some other great power, did in future seek a truly oppressive hegemony that would impose its system and values on Australia, then nuclear forces would make a decisive difference. They would decide whether Australia could preserve itself, its territory and its society against a major power that did seek to subdue its region in the way the aggressive dictatorships of the twentieth century did. No one can tell today how unlikely that scenario is.

The questions we face today about our future in Asia are not new. In different ways they have been with us for much of Australia's history, ever since Britain's power began to wane in the late nineteenth century. Indeed, the question of how we could make our way in Asia when we have no English-speaking protector has been implicit in our circumstances ever since the British first settled here, because it was always clear that the distribution of power and influence that made Britain ascendant in Asia might not last forever, and only in the past few decades have we succumbed to the agreeable illusion that American primacy would be any more permanent. So until recently we have always understood that one day the great powers of Asia – huge societies with powerful states and immense latent strength – would realise their potential and reclaim the leadership of their region from the hands of Western intruders, and that we would then have to find our place in the new Asia that would emerge. That's why our "fear of abandonment" has always been tinged with the recognition that our fears were bound to materialise one day. It has been ultimately a question of when, not if, and now we know the answer. The "when" is now.

It could have come much sooner. Over fifty years ago, in 1964, the thought that it had arrived provided the starting point for Donald Horne's *The Lucky Country*. In the prologue, subtitled "Peopled from all over Asia," Horne conjures Asia's rising power and wonders how Australia can possibly adapt as Britain and America fade. He sees this as the challenge that will test the "lucky country run mainly by second-rate people," whose "leaders ... so lack curiosity about the events that surround them that they are often taken by surprise." The whole book is framed as an enquiry into whether Australia has what it takes to pass this test and make its way in Asia alone. His conclusion was resoundingly ambivalent.

Australia turned out to be luckier than Horne could know. Within a decade of his book, Britain had gone from our region as a strategic power, but America remained – to everyone's surprise – stronger in Asia than ever. We did indeed prove to be the lucky country, as America's benign hegemony both kept us secure and underwrote the Asian economic miracle that made us prosperous. Countries with this kind of luck do not really need a foreign policy, because the world works well for them as it is. It is the unlucky ones that must struggle, making tough choices and hard sacrifices to shape the world around them as best they can to stay, or become, secure and prosperous. Now our luck is turning, and we must start taking foreign policy more seriously again.

As Horne saw, this will be a test of our national qualities. It is not clear that we are better placed to pass that test today than Horne thought we were in 1964. His mordant description of a "country run mainly by second-rate people," whose "leaders so lack curiosity ... that they are often taken by surprise," fits uncomfortably well today. In fact it may fit better today than it did back then. In the two decades after 1964, a lot was achieved to remake Australia, and Australia's place in Asia. Leaders abandoned the White Australia policy, opened to China, welcomed the Vietnamese boat people, adopted defence self-reliance, built a stable relationship with Indonesia, abandoned colonialism in the South Pacific, transformed key areas of our society, including health and education, made the first small but essential steps towards reconciliation, and began a radical reform of our economy which has been the foundation of our prosperity ever since. How does the record of the last twenty years compare with that?

Clearly we have made a very poor start. Historians looking back at our time will be puzzled by how complacently our political leaders have clung to their illusions about America's power when the evidence that things were changing has been so clear. Had they not done so, there is much that could have been done to make our position today stronger. They could have begun to build the armed forces we will need when we can no longer rely on the American alliance, rather than wasting billions on warship projects designed to win votes in Adelaide rather than battles at sea. They could have begun to build the relationship we will need with Indonesia in coming decades, rather than hold it hostage to third-order issues like people-smuggling. They could have begun quietly but firmly to set clear limits to what we are willing to allow China to do in our territory, instead of flipping, as we have done, between timidity and petulance.

Above all, they could have begun a serious conversation with Washington about America's future in Asia. Looking back from late 2017, it is hard to avoid the thought that we missed a big chance with Barack Obama. America was never going to do as Obama hoped and remain the uncontested leader of Asia indefinitely. But it could nonetheless have retained some significant strategic role, balancing and limiting China's power and influence, and that would have been greatly to Australia's benefit. It would have meant a new US role in Asia that maximised influence and minimised rivalry with China by making some significant concessions while holding firm to some non-negotiable principles. It would have required extraordinary feats of international statecraft and domestic politics to deliver, but Obama could have been the leader to do it. He never seems to have really engaged intellectually with Asia policy, perhaps because he was persuaded by his advisers that the Pivot was going to work. But things might have been different had he been persuaded by someone outside Washington that the Pivot wouldn't work, and that a more radical and creative approach was both necessary and possible. An effective Australian prime minister could have convinced him of that, had he or she had the insight to understand the issues and the courage to present them forcefully. Obama was the kind of president who might have listened, and acted. It is wrong to assume that Australia could never have had that kind of influence; how could we know if we've never tried? We will never know now, because it is too late. But we do know that the chance for America to build such a role was there, and has now passed, and Australia did nothing.

There is a warning in this. If we don't lift our game, we will fail to navigate the biggest shift in Australia's international circumstances since European settlement. The signs of failure are already clear, as we risk sliding straight from complacency to moral panic, so that our capacity to respond effectively is undermined by a growing assumption that even a relatively light version of Chinese primacy would pose a mortal threat to

Australia's values, interests and identity. We can see the signs of this panic in the implication of Malcolm Turnbull's Singapore speech that even a Monroe Doctrine model of Chinese regional leadership would be simply intolerable for Australia. In fact, it is far from clear that this is so – but if we assume it is, we will miss the chance to adapt to make the best of it.

That kind of failure might take several different forms. One would be to launch ourselves into a desperate and futile search for a new great and powerful friend to protect us from China as America fades. That would increase our vulnerability by entrapping us in others' disputes with China, while giving us little reason to expect their support in return. Another form of failure would be to give up and not even try to limit China's influence, even where there are clear options to do so. A third way to fail would be to flirt with the idea of defying geographic and economic reality by turning our back on an Asia that fell under China's sway. This might have seemed wildly improbable were it not for the example set by Britain's Brexit from Europe. It will be interesting to see whether Australia's political populists follow the example of their British counterparts and agitate for Australia to escape China's clutches by abandoning its economic opportunities and throwing our economic and strategic lot in with America, and perhaps with a post-Brexit Britain. It would be absurd, of course, but then again so is Brexit.

What would success look like? It would start, first, by acknowledging the problem, instead of denying it. It would also mean recognising that Australia's relative power in Asia has declined sharply, and is going to keep declining as Asian economies grow faster than ours. Today in Southeast Asia only Indonesia's economy is bigger than ours, but (on PwC's estimates) by 2050 Malaysia, Thailand, Vietnam and the Philippines will all have overtaken us. In 2050 China's economy will be twenty-three times larger than ours. Today America's is only sixteen times larger. But it would also mean recognising that we have some real and growing assets, including over 1 million Australians of Chinese descent. It is too easy to overlook the vital and obvious contribution they will make to helping us find our way in a Chinese-dominated East Asia. It would mean learning a lot more about China, thinking a lot more about how to influence it to our advantage, and reconciling in our own minds the conflicting imperatives that drive us in dealing with Beijing.

And it would mean recognising that we will change as a country as we adapt to the new Asia without America's support. We will become more Asian, of course – demographically, socially, culturally, diplomatically and strategically. That is a path we embarked upon a long time ago – back in Donald Horne's 1960s, in fact, with the end of White Australia – but we are perhaps a little less comfortable than we were a few decades ago about the reality that our identity as a country is changing, at least to judge by how our leaders talk. Would any of our leaders today speak of "Australia's Asian future" with Paul Keating's eager confidence? We need to recapture some of that confidence in our changing identity, because there is no going back, and the trends that drive us forward into Asia will accelerate and deepen when Asia is no longer dominated by Western powers.

None of this can be done without political leadership. We will not begin to adapt to the new Asia until our political leaders start to explain what is happening and to debate what we should do. It is not complicated. Someone – a prime minister or a leader of the Opposition, a foreign minister or a shadow foreign minister – just has to find the courage to say a few things that everyone knows, deep down, to be true.

China's rise is a fact and isn't going away. It constitutes a profound shift in the distribution of power in Asia, and is creating a new regional order in which China has a lot more influence, and America has less. America's future role cannot be taken for granted. It won't help to panic. Australia must adjust to this new order, by working out how we relate to China and working with other countries in Asia. This will require us to rethink a lot of things, to make some hard choices, and perhaps to pay some heavy costs. We will be changed in the process. Let's get on with it.

SOURCES

9   "Would you go to war?": Helene Cooper, "Patrolling disputed waters, US and China jockey for dominance", *New York Times*, 30 March 2016. General Dunford is the Chairman of the US Joint Chiefs of Staff. Admiral Harris is the Commander of US forces in the Pacific.

12   "has been expertly analysed": John Mearsheimer, *Tragedy of Great Power Politics*, New York: W.W. Norton, 2001; Graham Allison, *Destined for War: Can America and China escape Thucydides's Trap?* New York: Houghton Mifflin Harcourt, 2017.

13   "They all reluctantly": T.G. Otte. *The July Crisis: The World's Descent into War, Summer 1914*, Cambridge: Cambridge University Press, 2014.

15   "The United States is": Remarks by President Obama to the Australian Parliament, Canberra, 17 November 2011.

25   "In a remarkable interview": "The Obama Doctrine": The *Atlantic's* exclusive report on the US president's hardest foreign policy decisions", *Atlantic*, 10 March 2016.

31   "Accountancy firm PwC": PwC, *The Long View: How Will the Global Economic Order Change by 2050?* PwC (online), February 2017, p. 68.

41   "This possibility had loomed before": Adam Tooze, *The Deluge: The Great War and the Remaking of the World Order*, London: Penguin, 2014, esp. pp. 161ff.

42   "three real options": Hugh White, *The China Choice: Why America Should Share Power*, Melbourne: Black Inc., 2012, pp. 101ff.

42   "a number of scholars": Lyle Goldstein, *Meeting China Halfway: How to Defuse the Emerging US-China Rivalry*, Washington DC: Penguin, 2015; Michael D. Swaine, *Creating a Stable Asia : An Agenda for a US-China Balance of Power* Washington: Carnegie Endowment for International Peace, 2016; Charles Glaser, "A U.S.-China Grand Bargain? The Hard Choice between Military Competition and Accommodation", *International Security*, vol. 39, no. 4, 2015, pp. 49–90; Kevin Rudd, *U.S.-China 21 The Future of U.S.-China Relations Under Xi Jinping Toward a new Framework of Constructive Realism for a Common Purpose*, Harvard, 2015.

44   "keynote speech": Malcolm Turnbull, Keynote address 16th IISS Asia Security Summit Shangri-La Dialogue, Singapore, 2 June 2017.

45   "Australia's alliance": Shalailah Medora, "Tony Abbott says US defence official misspoke on B-1 bombers in Australia", *Guardian*, 15 May 2015.

45   "Howard himself has suggested": John Howard, *Lazarus Rising*, HarperCollins, Sydney, 2010, p. 502.

47   "There was bitter haggling": Bob Carr, *Diary of a Foreign Minister* Sydney 2014 pp. 142ff.

49   "a famous dressing down": David Wroe, "China's rebuke of Julie Bishop 'rudest' conduct seen in 30 years, says senior foreign affairs official", *Sydney Morning Herald*, 27 February 2014.

49   "Premier Li Keqiang warned": "Stay out of China's quarrels with us, Li Keqiang warn Australia", *Australian*, 24 March 2017.

50   "Which of these": Remarks by President Obama at the University of Queensland, Brisbane, 15 November 2014.

51   "an influential *Four Corners*": "Power and Influence", *Four Corners*, ABC TV, 5 June 2017.

52   "His abusive first phone call": "Donald Trump and Malcolm Turnbull's phone call: The full transcript", ABC Online, 4 August 2017.

52   "Turnbull's extraordinary decision": Malcolm Turnbull, radio interview with Neil Mitchell, AM, ABC Radio, 11 August 2017.

54   "Turnbull did at one time": Malcolm Turnbull, Speech at the launch of the 2011 PWC/Melbourne Institute AsiaLink Index, 28 November 2011.

54   "Penny Wong, as shadow foreign minister": Penny Wong, Speech at Future Asia: Engaging with China, Australian Institute of International Affairs Annual Conference, Canberra, 16 October 2017.

56   "the word 'self-reliance'": Hugh White, "DWP 2016 and self-reliance", *The Strategist* blog, Australian Strategic Policy Institute, 8 March 2016.

56   "that we should": Turnbull, 28 November 2011.

63   "by 2030 it is predicted": PwC, *The Long View*.

70   "In recent years": Evan A. Feigenbaum, "Is coercion the new normal in China's economic statecraft?", Marco Polo (online) 25 July 2017; Brahma Chellaney, "China's weaponisation of trade", *The Strategist* (blog), Australian Strategic Policy Institute, 28 July 2017.

71   "Over the past few years": David Wroe, "Chinese naval ships close to Australia? Get used to it, experts warn", *Sydney Morning Herald*, 10 March 2017.

75–6   "lucky country": Donald Horne, *The Lucky Country*, Melbourne: Penguin, 2005, pp. 1, 233.

79   "It would mean": This is discussed by Linda Jakobson and Bates Gill in *China Matters: Getting It Right for Australia*, La Trobe University Press, Melbourne 2017.

Lyle Shelton

Perhaps the biggest fault-line running through contemporary Western civilisation is where one stands on the cultural agenda of the LGBTIQ political movement. To have reservations is to be a bigot, unworthy of admission to polite society – an intellectual and social pariah.

As I write this, Australians are one month away from delivering their verdict on the redefinition of marriage in the Turnbull government's marriage postal survey conducted by the Australian Bureau of Statistics. Voters are continually told that Safe Schools, sex education and gender theory have nothing to do with the question of whether two people of the same gender (or anywhere on the spectrum of gender) should be allowed to marry. Benjamin Law's Quarterly Essay, *Moral Panic 101*, bells the cat, because in it Law admits what the "Yes" campaign has studiously denied – that same-sex marriage and Safe Schools are "the country's two biggest LGBTIQ issues."

Law praises Labor for its commitment to both. Labor, under Bill Shorten, has pledged to legislate same-sex marriage within 100 days of its election and to fund the so-called Safe Schools program from the Commonwealth purse. By contrast, the federal Coalition is split on both Safe Schools and same-sex marriage. The outcome of the postal vote will be critical to both issues.

Honest "Yes" campaigners, like Law, know that same-sex marriage and Safe Schools are a package deal. "It might be stating the obvious," he writes, "but same-sex marriage is far from the final frontier in the battle against homophobia." Law's argument that "Safe Schools should be implemented in every school" certainly projects that frontier well beyond the comfort levels of most parents, even those who might otherwise be amenable to a redefinition of marriage.

That same-sex marriage and Safe Schools are joined at the hip is confirmed by the experience of countries such as the United States and Canada, where same-sex marriage has either been legislated or imposed by the courts. People forget that the "T" in LGBTIQ stands for "transgender." Justine Greening, the UK minister for equality in Theresa May's Conservative government, said people being able to legally change their gender was the next "step forward" after same-sex marriage was legalised in 2013. Men identifying as women in the UK must now be allowed into women's private spaces, regardless of whether they have had gender-reassignment surgery. An ideology built on queer theory and that proposes gender is fluid and detached from biology must then be taught in schools. In this way, "advances" in transgender rights and "bathroom wars" entail an equivalent loss of parents' rights to say "No" to their children being exposed to Safe Schools–style programs.

In Australia, believing same-sex marriage was inevitable, the LGBTIQ political movement got ahead of itself and began rolling out Safe Schools prematurely, exposing parents for the first time to the movement's ideology – a preview of what awaits on the other side of the rainbow. This has understandably caused "moral panic" among many parents – something for which Law despises them. Parents who object are pilloried as so many Helen Lovejoys (the *Simpsons* character who hysterically and irrationally cries, "Won't someone think of the children!?").

As difficult as it is for Law and the LGBTIQ political movement to understand, millions of parents are not on board with their children being told, as youth organisation Minus18 states, that "there are two virginities," or that "penis and vagina sex is not the only sex and certainly not the ultimate sex." Most parents do not believe that gender is on a spectrum and has nothing to do with one's genitalia and would be concerned that children in schools can be affirmed as the opposite gender, setting them on a pathway to damaging puberty blockers, cross-sex hormones and irreversible sex-change surgery, with or without parental consent. Chest-binding for girls and penis-tucking for boys is not every Australian mother and grandmother's vision for the flourishing of their children.

Yet Law's essay assumes and asserts that parents who resist this are at best homophobic or transphobic and, at worst, complicit in causing the suicide of young people. It is the use of child suicide as an emotional battering ram that makes the debate difficult for all people of goodwill to navigate. No one wants to see children bullied or commit suicide. Yet, if LGBTIQ activists like Law are to be believed, to disagree with same-sex marriage and programs like Safe Schools is the moral equivalent of bullying or having blood on your hands.

Indeed, Westpac sent an email to thousands of its employees urging them to vote "Yes" to same-sex marriage because that would prevent 3000 gay suicides per year. Never mind that this exceeded the total number of deaths by suicide annually for all Australians. Never mind that while suicidal ideation and attempts appear to be higher among gay people, claims that "completed" suicide rates for the LGBT community are higher are only speculative. Never mind that same-sex marriage has not been a panacea to gay suicide or suicidal ideation in the small number of countries that have changed their laws.

When Brisbane schoolboy Tyrone Unsworth took his life, many on Twitter blamed me. Law begins his essay detailing the news reports of his tragic death, musing that if Aspley High School had been a Safe School, Unsworth might still be with us. An inconvenient truth ignored in the debate about Safe Schools is that studies reveal the suicide mortality rate for transgender people ten years after a sex-change operation is still twenty times higher than for the non-transgender population. Suicide rates among homosexual married couples remain significantly higher than for heterosexual married couples. These studies are from gay- and transgender-friendly Sweden. They contradict the assertion that social stigma is the single contributing factor to reduced mental health for the LGBTIQ community. You won't read about this on Education Minister Simon Birmingham's Student Wellbeing Hub, where the Safe Schools resources have migrated since the Commonwealth defunded the program.

I am on a unity ticket with Law when it comes to bullying. No one should be called "faggot," "poof" or "tranny," and no one should be subjected to violence. It hardly needs saying that there should be no bashings and murders of gay people. These have always been my beliefs, not in spite of but because of my upbringing as a Christian – a religion Law assumes is intrinsically hostile to gay people. But having love in one's heart towards people, which is a command of Christ, does not preclude disagreement on public policy or on the highly questionable "science" of gender theory.

Law assumes that gender theory is not theory. He asserts it as fact because it is the lived experience of some people. As in Hans Christian Andersen's story "The Emperor's New Clothes," anyone who disagrees with the new "Truth" must be a fool. However, the same story reminds us that majority affirmation of a false belief does not make it factual. In Law's mind, the "facts" of gender theory mean the debate about whether or not gender is on a spectrum is over. It is only the clueless who look at the genitalia of a baby and "assign" a gender accordingly. Safe Schools promotes a resource for four-year-olds, *The Gender Fairy*, by Jo Hirst, which tells children, "only you can know if you are a boy or a girl, no one can tell you" – not Mummy or Daddy and certainly not the bigoted doctor who presided at your birth. Never mind that archaeologists can still identify ancient bones as belonging to either a man or a woman and that no amount of puberty blockers, cross-sex hormones or surgery can alter mitochondrial DNA. What it means to be a man or a woman may be up for debate, but the binary nature of gender is biologically hardwired into every human creature's chromosomes.

A minuscule percentage of people are born with ambiguous genitalia and this causes distress for many of these people. A small number of people, including children, experience mental anguish because they strongly feel that they are trapped in the wrong body. Compassion requires we support these people. None of this means children should be encouraged to "transition" at school, as Safe Schools recommends. If left alone, the overwhelming majority of children who experience distress about their gender will, by the time they get through puberty, reorient to their biological sex.

The thing that has caused many parents to panic in the wake of each new revelation about Safe Schools material is that it was introduced to schools without parental consent and thrives by keeping them in the dark. As Law points out, signing on to Safe Schools occurs when a principal does so: there is no requirement to consult with parents. Indeed, Safe Schools co-founder Roz Ward boasted that parents were powerless to stop it. She recommended that schools respond to parental concerns by saying: "We're doing it anyway. Tough luck."

LGBTIQ politics does not accept that parents have the right to have the final say on the education of their children. This has been the experience of parents like Steve Tourloukis of Ontario, Canada, after same-sex marriage was legalised. He lost a Supreme Court case where he fought for the right to have his children withdrawn from radical LGBTIQ sex education classes. It is the experience, after same-sex marriage was legalised, of the Vishnitz Jewish school in London, which has now failed three Ofsted tests because it refuses to teach LGBTIQ sex education.

Despite a United Nations affirmation of the right of parents to educate their children as they see fit, including in their religion, in Law's worldview parents who do not accept that gender is on a spectrum are a danger to their children. The LGBTIQ political movement, which sees dissenting parents as harmful to children, needs to be upfront with parents about what rights they will or will not have if LGBTIQ political agendas are adopted by governments.

Law is right that Australians have come a long way in their tolerance of the LGBTIQ community and that is not a bad thing. But acceptance of people does not mean parents have to accept a school system that teaches all children that their gender is fluid or that, sexually, anything goes. Most parents want the freedom for their boys to be boys, their girls to be girls and for all kids to enjoy the innocence of childhood. An LGBTIQ view of the world makes that impossible. Redefining marriage in law makes that impossible.

Law quotes former ACT Greens convenor Simon Copland, who advocates for marriage equality to be extended to polygamous relationships. People like Law and Copland are admirable for being honest in the extrapolation of the logic of their ideas, something the "Yes" campaign for same-sex marriage studiously avoids. Words like "bigot," "homophobe," "hater" and the use of suicide have been powerful weapons to discourage scrutiny and to intimidate those who question LGBTIQ political ideas. The conflation of legitimate concerns about the ill-treatment of gay people and people struggling with gender dysphoria with homophobia or transphobia have been used to leap-frog science and silence the public discussion necessary to democracy.

Knowing the truth about the political agenda of the LGBTIQ movement, the Coalition for Marriage, of which I am a director, raised the impact on education as a consequence of same-sex marriage. The publication of Law's essay, and his explicit acknowledgment of the connection between same-sex marriage and Safe Schools, is a further and well-timed validation of our campaign's concerns. As Heidi McIvor (one of the mums who appeared in our television ads) has said: "Our children are not your social experiment." Whether or not LGBTIQ politics continues its march through our classrooms will depend on whether Australian parents accept Law's view that they have no rights when it comes to programs like Safe Schools, and on whether they have any grounds to oppose such programs if marriage is redefined.

Lyle Shelton

Amy Middleton

I was aware of my sexuality, and my non-heterosexual orientation, from about eight years of age. This childhood sexual awareness didn't come from any outside force: my parents had explained the basics and given me a copy of *Where Did I Come From?* but it was still about five years before I'd receive any classroom teaching about sex, desire or anatomy.

I found this early sexual awareness confusing and distressing; I was an observant kid, and very aware of how constrained everyone became when the subject of sex was raised. When I took this distress to my mum, she was informative and compassionate, and urged me to honour my instincts. Unsurprisingly, my distress eased when I received guidance and information in place of awkwardness and silence.

This kind of experience is very relevant to the debate around Safe Schools. I believe educational resources on sex and gender should be available for school-age kids. Diversity starts young, and ignoring that fact can be dangerous for some kids, even life-threatening.

The advocates for silence around diversity – the journalists, politicians and pundits who fear the impact of such frank discussions with children – are not the individuals most affected by this debate or its outcome. The success of Benjamin Law's essay lies in his observation that although these hostile voices may be the loudest, they are far from the most crucial.

My anecdote also speaks to a truth identified in *Moral Panic 101*: "The notion of transgender children neatly braids some of our biggest anxieties ... we don't want kids prematurely sexualised." Of course, kids and sex can be a frightening mix: it can be hard to know when to open up and when to remain quiet. But the individual who stands to suffer the most from fear, hesitation and silence around sexuality and gender is the child. As Law points out, we – the parents, politicians, teachers or journalists – should be grown-up enough to handle our own fear and discomfort, in order to better protect those looking to us for help.

Law also astutely observes that the arguments from both sides of this debate have something in common. On one hand, there are those concerned for children who identify as gay, lesbian, bisexual, transgender and intersex and the statistically poor mental health outcomes they currently face in Australia. On the other, there are those concerned for children growing up in a society that challenges traditional notions of sex and gender, and what that might mean for their development. Both sides are worried about the welfare of children, and yet this essay is one of the first widely circulated reports on this issue that includes real anecdotes – like the one I've shared above – from the very children we are all apparently trying to protect.

If we all agree that children's welfare is at the heart of this debate, then surely their perspectives are important. If you believe kids lack the maturity to know what they need in terms of information, we should then be listening to the people on the front-lines – those with lived experience of identifying as LGBTIQ, those who have guided them through their journeys, and the experts most familiar with issues of sexual and gender diversity in children. It seems those on the front-lines were largely unmoved by the media-fuelled furore around Safe Schools: as Law reports, the number of principals signing up to the program continued to climb throughout the media storm.

Law's is also the first report to detail what was *actually* rolled out as part of the Safe Schools program. As it turns out, there is no curriculum. There is no mandatory teaching. All it requires is a pledge to work towards promoting feelings of safety among a group of vulnerable kids. And what's offered is a bunch of optional resources and an elective teacher training course. This is not a radical commitment, no matter which side of the debate you're on; it's an opportunity for schools to take steps that might save the lives of kids like Tyrone Unsworth.

As a journalist, I'm a passionate believer in the value of personal stories as a means to tease out complex issues – the bulk of my work as publisher of *Archer Magazine* involves sharing lesser-heard voices on the subject of sex and gender. Now in its tenth print edition, *Archer Magazine* has amassed a community of readers more fiercely loyal and loving than I could have imagined when I founded the publication back in 2013. The audience is niche, but that's of no real consequence: tens of thousands of readers have attached themselves firmly to this masthead because they seek support and representation from the media. *Archer's* LGBTIQ-focused stories offer solidarity in a world that often tells us we are unwelcome or not accepted.

Journalists and editors have a duty of care to provide space for these voices where possible, or, at an absolute minimum, to avoid denigrating them to the point of causing harm. *Moral Panic 101* depicts a conservative newspaper conducting a despicable, relentless scare campaign about Safe Schools – a crusade that flatly ignored the very real risks involved in its line of attack. The safety of LGBTIQ kids is too serious an issue to become a political ping-pong ball or a media power-play. The focus in discussions of Safe Schools should always have been the wellbeing of the individuals who need the program most. According to the National LGBTI Health Alliance, LGBTIQ children are at far more likely to self-harm or experience depression and are five times more likely to attempt suicide than straight cisgender children. Protecting their welfare and respecting their experiences is fundamental in ethical journalism, and this responsibility was shamefully disregarded in the media storm around Safe Schools.

It isn't easy for members of the wider community to put themselves in the shoes of people experiencing oppression. In October I wrote an article for the *Sydney Morning Herald* about what it feels like to be pregnant and in a same-sex relationship during the marriage equality postal survey. The article was shared widely and I was inundated with messages from friends and allies expressing sadness and frustration on my behalf. I was surprised by their surprise – for me, the impact of this debate is bordering on banal. The feeling that my sexuality is a discussion point for the nation, seeing people campaigning against my rights in my own neighbourhood – these are unsettling and humiliating experiences, but this is my life. My community is intimately familiar with these sorts of experiences and understands their effects.

The reaction to my article reminded me that others can't possibly share this perspective, and that voices like mine are especially crucial right now. Similarly, in the discussion of Safe Schools the voices of trans kids, experts and those directly engaging with the Safe Schools program are crucial. Far less important are the voices of overbearing politicians with abject opinions, religious lobbyists with fearful predictions, and journalists drumming up public outcry through factual inaccuracies and fear-mongering.

I'm grateful to Benjamin Law for separating fact from falsehood, and for holding the media to account for causing harm to a vulnerable group. Most of all, I commend him for amplifying the voices that are truly crucial in this discussion, over those that, frankly, we could stand to hear from a lot less.

Amy Middleton

Dennis Altman

For those of my generation there's a bittersweet tang to reading Ben's essay. As he reminds us, difference in sexual identity or gender expression has been the target for persecution, discrimination and hate throughout our lifetimes, and there are significant forces, both religious and political, determined to perpetuate this. The moral panic to which the essay refers is one in a long series of similar attacks on anyone seen to threaten the taken-for-granted assumptions of rigid gender and sexual binaries.

I am writing this during the increasingly heated campaign around same-sex marriage, almost certainly the most expensive opinion poll in history. I can only imagine the scene in the government party room after the results are posted, and the rush from both sides of a bitterly divided party to assure us that their side has won.

The question that Ben's essay pushes us to ask is whether there have been fundamental and irreversible changes towards acceptance of sexual and gender diversity. As he demonstrates, the assault on the Safe Schools program was part of a larger ideological push by the Murdoch press and the right wing of the governing parties to defend cultural values they claim are under threat. In the current debate on marriage, the spectre of Safe Schools undermining gender roles is a constant theme, and one that the Turnbull government has allowed to grow unfettered.

Any respect I might have had for the current prime minister was lost when, following the conclusion of an inquiry into the Safe Schools program by Minister Birmingham, Turnbull ignored its recommendations and announced the program would end anyway.

The opponents of Safe Schools are both opportunists and true believers, but social change has blunted their rhetoric. Even opponents of the LGBTI movement feel impelled to proclaim that they are against any form of bullying, and that they recognise the worth of same-sex relationships. When Reverend Fred Nile, our last remaining Old Testament prophet, proclaimed on *Q&A* last year that homosexuality should be recriminalised, even his supporters gasped.

As Ben suggests, fear of gender fluidity rather than homosexuality has become the rallying point for the right. One might point out that the carefully choreographed images of lesbian and gay male couples produced by the equality movement almost always reinforce conventional gender stereotypes, but in the popular imagination the categories blur, and most of us live happily with that confusion.

But not, it seems, Tony Abbott, the Catholic Church or the busy cultural warriors at the *Australian*. Ben points to the volume of stories they have produced on the threat of Safe Schools, but the story of harassment by media and threats to anyone associated with the program goes even further than he indicates. In a time of dying journalism, the resources employed to police gender in our schools suggest we are dealing with a threat second only to rapacious international terrorism.

Having assured us that marriage is not a primary concern for most voters, the *Australian* gives it constant attention, even though some of its regular columnists have been advocating for a "Yes" vote. Ben attributes this to a desire for readers and for political muscle. I think there is a third dimension, which is the panic felt by many believing Christians that the world they have known is collapsing around them.

At the official launch of the "No" campaign, former Liberal Cory Bernardi insisted that he was on the right side of history. His team has seized upon religious freedom to justify opposition to both marriage equality and Safe Schools, although it is never clear exactly what religious freedoms are threatened. What they really fear is the loss of an unchallenged Christian hegemony, supported by the state, despite protestations that ours is a secular society.

David Marr has regularly pointed to the many ways our political system favours organised religion. The school chaplains program, which would seem to contradict the basic assumptions of a secular state, remains well funded by the same government that axed Safe Schools (although the current agreement expires next year). The largest source of school chaplains is Access Ministries, which describes itself as "an ecumenical body committed to the basic doctrines of the Christian faith."

OECD data shows that Australia has an unusually high proportion of students in private education, which is overwhelmingly religious. How far anti-discrimination laws apply to religious schools is complex, but anecdotal evidence suggests that deep-seated prejudices against any form of sexual or gender deviance is common in fundamentalist schools of all faiths.

In understanding the passion to preserve conventional assumptions of sex and gender we should not underestimate the strength of religious belief within the Liberal Party. That the Victorian Liberals have switched from backing Safe Schools to opposition reflects a wider shift, namely the growth of religious fundamentalist influences within the party.

I am writing this as passions on both sides of the marriage debate become increasingly bitter and polarised. But there is a false equation here: those who are persecuted do not begin from the same position as those who persecute. Unlike a referendum on becoming a republic, this is not a debate in which everybody has an equal stake.

The underlying theme of Safe Schools is one of inclusion, of allowing a safe space to kids who are discovering that their sexuality or gender identity differs from that of early-evening commercial television. One of the striking aspects of the marriage debate is how many people say that it has unleashed memories of bullying, subterfuge and fear from their school days.

The first Quarterly Essay appeared in 2001; this is the first essay to be devoted to unpacking the fraught politics of sexuality, specifically of homophobia, in our history. But as with politicians like Barack Obama and Julia Gillard, who became strong advocates for same-sex marriage, one welcomes the latecomers.

Dennis Altman

John Whitehall

In his essay *Moral Panic 101*, Mr Law puzzled me with the declaration, "We might need to acknowledge something uncomfortable: that everyone ... wants the same thing: to keep kids safe." I wondered if this was a loose statement in an otherwise tightly controlled exposition. But a few lines further on, he declares, "Australian queers are impatient for change, seeing one kid's suicide attempt as one too many." Is he implying queers are the only ones upset? Allow me to reassure. In over fifty years of practising paediatric medicine in Australia, I am yet to meet a therapist uncommitted to the safety of children.

I do not deny space for queers in the ranks of those concerned about children. However, with regard to the cause, diagnosis and management of gender dysphoria, I have a different view to some, including Mr Law. He regards the Safe Schools program as a solution; I see it as a problem.

Mr Law declares his essay is intended for those "baffled" why commentators are still "railing against a queer 'agenda' or 'ideology,' something that would sound anachronistically quaint if it wasn't so nakedly hateful." I confess I am baffled by this rhetoric. Does he mean it is now anachronistic to critique ideologies in general? Or is he proclaiming that queer theory has so evolved from disputed discourse to established science that all critique is now historically and chronologically misplaced? If the former, is civilisation now to forget the cost of other utopian ideologies? Mr Law admits he has been visiting China. Do the millions of victims of the theories of Marx, Lenin and Mao Zedong give no warning that ideas have consequences? If the latter, what need is there to attempt to suppress questioning with emotive accusations of hatred? Or is Mr Law merely using high-sounding words to dismiss those who disagree with queer theory as hateful troglodytes?

Mr Law may have provided insight in his objection to News Corp newspapers dismissing queer theory as mere "theory." Apparently in defence, Mr Law explains that "queer theory is an intellectual discourse and critical theory – and not a theory in the scientific sense" and concludes that to declare otherwise is "cute and wilful misreading."

I am not sure what to make of this in the context of childhood gender dysphoria. It would appear that on the confessedly unscientific basis of certain ideas, Mr Law would have us accept that gender identity is fluid, inconstant and flexible, despite the physical reality that half of us have two X chromosomes and the other an X and a Y, and that these arrangements have denoted sexual difference that has procreated the world in which we live. Whether we believe God created Man and Woman or that they emerged from primordial soup, this binary arrangement has a scientific basis and obeys scientific laws. When we teach children otherwise, we are preaching alchemy. When we castrate children on the basis of those ideas, it is anything but "cute."

I reject the idea that "intersex," otherwise known as disorders of sex development, is relevant to the discussion of gender dysphoria. Law repeats Roz Ward's claim that 1.7 per cent of the population is so affected: this is propagation of unscientific exaggeration, if not recruitment of the suffering of rare disease for ideological purpose.

Childhood gender dysphoria, once rare, is now epidemic. Even long-running, well-known gender identity clinics, such as that at the Centre for Addiction and Mental Health in Toronto, used not to have many clients, but now hundreds of children are being brought to special clinics in Australian capital cities each year. A professor consulted in a recent Family Court case for a twelve-year-old seeking drugs to delay puberty, Re Brodie (Special Medical Procedure), was asked why numbers of children seeking treatment had previously been very low. He concluded, "They just suffer out there, I think."

I dispute that conclusion. I asked twenty-eight general paediatricians with a cumulative experience of 931 years and they could recall only twelve cases of childhood gender dysphoria: ten associated with severe mental disease, and two with severe physical abuse. Given paediatricians are privy to parental concerns regarding all kinds of sexual behaviour in children, it is hard to imagine that gender confusion would not have been confided.

What has caused the epidemic? Given there is no virus or substance that could cause such discord with natal sex, the reason must be psychological. I conclude it is a phenomenon driven by the media and the internet, and delivered to the immature mind with the imprimatur of the school. I believe it is a contagious social fad that infects both children and parents.

Of course there have been social fads before and many have been harmless, but gender dysphoria may incur a lasting cost, depending on the treatment, for which there are three options.[1] The first is active dissuasion, the second "watchful waiting," and the third a medical pathway. This medical path begins with social transitioning, progresses to the blocking of puberty, then to the administration of cross-sex hormones, then to surgical attempts to create the ersatz external characteristics of the opposite sex. Known as the "Dutch protocol," it is a massive intrusion into the mind and body of children, though performed with the best of intentions.

Does this intrusion make the child happier? No one knows in the long term. One of many problems for long-term happiness is the prevalence of associated mental disorders, including autism, which features in more than half of my review of cases of childhood gender dysphoria which have appeared before the Family Court of Australia since 2004. This high prevalence is confirmed in reviews from leading international centres.[2] Some argue the associated mental disorder is secondary to gender dysphoria, but others reveal it preceded the gender confusion.

Does the medical pathway reduce the likelihood of self-harm? Again, no one knows. There is no doubt that sufferers from discord between mind and body deserve help and treatment. But it is an experimental concept that an autistic youth from a broken home might be less likely to self-harm by fostering the illusion he belongs to the opposite sex. It is known, however, that the suicide rate in adults who have undergone sex reassignment surgery is very much higher than in the general population,[3] strongly suggesting the best way to avoid suicide is to avoid the medical pathway.

Is the medical pathway safe? Here Mr Law appears to accept the assurance of therapists, unaware of the warning of the High Court of Australia in *Secretary Department of Health and Community Services v JWB and SMB* (1992) against unqualified trust in the medical profession: "Like all professions, the medical profession has members who are not prepared to live up to its professional standards of ethics ... Further, it is also possible that members of that profession may form sincere but misguided views about the appropriate steps to be taken."

Undoubtedly sincere, members of the profession have nevertheless failed to inform the family courts of Australia about possible side effects of their medical pathway on the growing brain. Perhaps therapists are unaware of current medical literature, but surely such invasive and irreversible interventions warrant continued review of this? Perhaps a sensitivity acquired in clinical practice leads to a preference for the more delicate term of "reduced fertility" than the C word (castration), in discussion of the effects of cross-sex hormones and surgical reassignment. Even Mr Law softens the concept of bilateral mastectomy by introducing the more delicate notion of "reducing breast size."

Regarding puberty blockers, Mr Law reports therapists "have been using this reversible method for a decade now," to buy time in which the child receives psychological support. But science suggests these blockers are not safe to use. Puberty involves sequential release of a chain of hormones (or chemical messengers), which begins deep in the brain and eventually triggers release of the sex hormones (oestrogen and testosterone), which end in development of characteristic male and female features.

Almost four decades ago, the hormone GnRH was isolated and chemically identified, permitting the manufacture of an analogue that would stimulate the pituitary, but would not "let go" of the receptors, preventing a "recharging" of the gland, resulting in its exhaustion, and thus causing puberty to stall for as long as it was administered.

With the discovery of GnRH, scientists wondered if it had other physiological jobs to do. Ultimately, evidence of GnRH activity was revealed in many centres in the brain,[4] spinal cord, and intestinal neurons.[5] What would happen to those functions if blockers were administered?

Concerns about the widespread effect of blockers rose with their use in adult women and men who were suffering from diseases stimulated by their sex hormones: for example, adult men with prostate cancer. In such cases, a strong suggestion arose of interference with executive brain function, demanding further investigation.[6] In animal laboratories in Scotland and Norway, sheep were given blockers, which were found to lead to swelling of the area of the brain that integrates emotions, learning, thinking and memory.[7] This swelling was associated with abnormal function of many of the genes of the amygdala and, not surprisingly, sustained reduction in emotional stability and memory. The effects in both adults and peripubertal sheep were discerned after short periods of administration. Transgendering children, however, may receive blockers for years, spanning an intense period of brain growth.[8]

Blockers are given to peripubertal children to afford them more time for consideration of gender identity, free of distraction from the development of secondary sex characteristics. But, first, is it reasonable to expect any pubertal child to be able to understand and predict their sexual and reproductive future? Second, is such contemplation valid when the brain has been damaged by chemicals? Third, is it reasonable to expect a child to comprehend a sexual future when their brain, ordained in foetal life to await activation by a certain hormone, receives one it was not expecting? Everything points to continued confusion and yet pursuit of the next step in the pathway.

That step is the administration of cross-sex hormones and, again, medical therapists have under-informed the courts. Certainly, lists of side effects have been proffered and warnings have been given of reduced fertility, but the court has yet to be advised of the effect of cross-sex hormones on the structure of the brain. The brains of transgender males on oestrogen have been shown to shrink at a rate ten times faster than ageing. Natal females on testosterone have demonstrated abnormal enlargement of the grey matter due to the anabolic effect of testosterone.[9] No one knows the long-term outcome of marinating the developing adolescent brain in such chemicals.

Is the medical pathway necessary? Mr Law criticises the American Psychiatric Association's *Diagnostic and Statistical Manual of Mental Disorders* (DSM-5), which states the majority of children with gender dysphoria will grow out of it. He dismisses its findings, declaring it is "loose with its figures." Certainly, DSM-5 reports a statistical range of the numbers of children desisting from confusion, but this confirms the overall lack of science regarding childhood gender dysphoria. Very little is fact. Intervention is, therefore, experimental. Mr Law dismisses my next two references because the numbers are too small. I agree the numbers are small but believe that smallness in those two centres of international renown substantiates two of my points. The first is that (until recently) gender dysphoria was rare. The second is that outcome is unpredictable. So why submit a child to medical intervention?

Perhaps Mr Law and I can compromise. If, for argument's sake, I accept the assertion that 1.2 to 4 per cent of adolescents report being transgender or gender-variant (which I do not) and he the assertion of the American Psychiatric Association that 0.002 to 0.014 per cent of the adult population seek help for transgender issues (which he may not), then we have both arrived at good news! Mathematics assures us that over 99.5 per cent of confused adolescents will no longer feel the need to seek help as adults. All we have to do is make sure we don't mess them up along the way. We need to be supportive, compassionate and patient, and avoid irreversible medical intervention. This is not to neglect other symptoms: depression and autism may need sustained care.

As a paediatrician, I am touched by Mr Law's apparent faith in my profession. He asks incredulously, "Where are the reckless medical professionals willing to perform needless interventions?" I have already referred to the failure of some of my colleagues to adequately inform the courts. I might share another disappointment.

Since expressing cynicism about medical intervention for childhood gender dysphoria, I have increasingly heard from concerned parents, here and overseas. In these contacts, several refrains are repeated. The first is the perfunctory assessment by questionnaire, which according to one mother merely reinforced confusion with such directive questions as "When did you first think you were of the opposite sex?" Then follows discussion (described as very short) with the child. Then the family is gathered for the proclamation, "You [parents] should say goodbye to your daughter and welcome your new son." Then, there is usually a pause for the parents to gather composure, followed by the offering of counselling – to the parents, not the child. One set of parents swears that after only fifteen minutes of interview, their sixteen-year-old child with a mental age of ten was introduced to the particulars of the Dutch protocol for medical transitioning. Such accounts cause me to wonder if more care is taken with the diagnosis and management of appendicitis than with the initiation of life-transforming gender therapy. Assurances reported by Mr Law that dysphoric children are "are professionally assessed" seem less plausible than parental concerns of recklessness.

Mr Law wonders how a "minor could manipulate the Family Court into allowing surgeons, psychiatrists and endocrinologists to perform needless medical acts on them." The minor is usually but one member of a committed team. With almost evangelical certitude they assert suffering is to be relieved, suicide avoided. What judge could resist? But there is more to this story. In eleven of sixty-nine recent court cases, the child was acknowledged to be unable to understand what was going on, and the decision to enter the medical pathway was made in his or her "best interests."

It is not "anachronistically quaint" to remind Mr Law that both lawyers and doctors have at times been sincerely committed to "needless medical acts." The eugenics movement in America at one time had widespread support; so too frontal lobotomies – in fact, their inventor, Egaz Monis, was awarded the Nobel Prize in Medicine in 1949.

Mr Law assures us that it is "nearly impossible for minors to undergo surgical procedures ... however ... there have been a handful of cases of ... transgender males surgically reducing breast size or undergoing bilateral mastectomies with court approval," and these are "rare enough" to make national news. Of the sixty-nine recent cases seeking court authorisation for irreversible transgender therapy, forty-four were natal females. Of these, five (that is, more than 10 per cent) had their breasts removed. Hardly impossible. Hardly rare.

Mr Law may be encouraged by the declaration of one therapist that "all cases she has ever read or heard of ... regretting treatment for gender dysphoria have been adults who have transitioned later in life, not minors on hormonal interventions." Given that the medical pathway for children with gender dysphoria is only recent, there has been little time for regrets. Nevertheless, I am reliably informed of two instances: a natal girl on testosterone disillusioned by hair on her chest, and a natal male on oestrogen disillusioned by breasts on his chest. Given the epidemic of gender dysphoria, as adolescents age, the numbers of disillusioned will surely increase.

Given the power of influence teachers have on a young mind, the Safe Schools program is making things worse. If we accept, as Mr Law insists, that queer theory is not based on science, what are we to call such forceful propagation of ideas if not propaganda?

Lastly, I would like to assure Mr Law that "we" as adult parents are not terrified we "may not control (the) destiny of our children." Most of us are keen to hand over agency to our children in their pursuit of independence. In the meantime, we see it as our duty to minimise harmful influences, including intellectual discourses that claim fantasy as fact.

John Whitehall

1 For more information, including references, see J. Whitehall, "Gender dysphoria and surgical abuse", *Quadrant*, December 2016; "Childhood gender dysphoria and the law", *Quadrant*, May 2017; and "The Family Court must protect gender-dysphoric children", *Quadrant*, November 2017.

2 R. Kaltiala-Heino, M. Sumia, M. Tyolajarvi, N. Lindberg, "Two years of gender identity service for minors: Overrepresentation of natal girls with severe problems in adolescent development", *Child and Adolescent Psychiatry and Mental Health*, vol. 9, no. 9, 2015.

3 M.H. Murad, M.B. Elamin, M.Z. Garcia, R.J. Mullan, A. Murad, P.J. Erwin & V.M. Montori, "Hormonal therapy and sex reassignment: A systematic review and meta-analysis of quality of life and psychosocial outcomes", *Clinical Endocrinology*, vol. 72, no. 2, 2010, pp. 214–31; C. Dhejne, P. Lichtenstein, M. Boman et al., "Long-term follow-up of transsexual persons undergoing sex reassignment surgery: Cohort study in Sweden", *Plos One*, vol. 6, no. 2, 2011.

4 E.G. Stopa, E.T. Koh, C.N. Svendsen, W.T. Rogers, J.S. Schwaber, J.C. King, "Computer-assisted mapping of immunoreactive mammalian gonadotropin-releasing hormone in adult human basal forebrain and amygdala", *Endocrinology*, vol. 128, no. 6, June 1991, pp. 3199–3207.

5 B. Ohlsson, "Gonadotropin-Releasing hormone and its role in the enteric nervous system", *Frontiers in Endocrinology*, no. 8, 7 June 2017, p. 110.

6 C.J. Nelson, J.S. Lee, M.C. Gamboa, A.J. Roth, "Cognitive effects of hormone therapy in men with prostate cancer: A review", *Cancer*, 2008 vol. 113, no. 5, 1 Sep 2008, pp. 1097–106;

M. Grigorova, B.B. Sherwin, T. Tulandi, "Effects of treatment with leuprolide acetate depot on working memory and executive functions in young premenopausal women", *Psychoneuroendocrinology*, vol. 31, no. 8, 2006, pp. 935–47.

7   S. Nuruddin, A. Krogenaes, et al. "Peri-pubertal gonadotropin-releasing hormone agonist treatment affects hippocampus gene expression without changing spatial orientation in young sheep", *Behavioural Brain Research*, no. 242, 2012, pp. 9–16; D. Hough, M. Bellingham, I.R. Haraldsen, et al., "A reduction in long-term spatial memory persists after discontinuation of peripubertal GnRH agonist treatment in sheep", *Psychoneuroendocrinology*, no. 77, March 2017, pp. 1–8.

8   Nuruddin et al., 2012.

9   L. Zubiaurre-Elorza, C. Junque, E. Gomez-Gil & A. Guillamon, "Effects of cross-sex hormone treatment on cortical thickness in transsexual individuals", *Journal of Sexual Medicine*, vol. 11, no. 5, May 2014, pp. 1248–61.

Scott Ryan

As the Parliamentary Secretary for Education from September 2013 to September 2015, I was directed to manage the government's relationship with the Foundation for Young Australians, which was delivering the Safe Schools program.

Benjamin Law interviewed me for his Quarterly Essay and recorded my "misgivings" about the program. However, he went on to misrepresent me and the steps I took.

In an unattributed statement, he wrote, "After the launch, Scott Ryan took his nascent concerns about Safe Schools to a Liberal party-room meeting but was rebuffed by Tony Abbott and Education Minister Christopher Pyne."

This statement is incorrect and was not verified by me or my staff, despite having been in contact with Benjamin a number of times for the essay.

While the convention holds that MPs do not talk about what happens in the party room, it is widely known, and has been previously reported, that this matter was raised and discussed in 2014 and 2015. However, I did not raise this matter in the party room. It would not have been appropriate for me, as then Parliamentary Secretary, to do so. The issue of the Safe Schools program was raised by several of my colleagues.

In government, the Coalition has put in place a number of anti-bullying and youth programs to address the challenges of youth mental health and bullying. From the appointment of a Children's e-Safety Commissioner to the expansion of the Headspace network, the Coalition government has committed to addressing these challenges across the health and education spectrum and continues to do so.

Most importantly, I support the need to teach all children that bullying and abuse, whether in person or online, can have a real impact and has no place. However, I did not see Safe Schools as the best way to achieve that, nor that the Commonwealth was well positioned to fund, manage and direct such a program.

Scott Ryan

Louis Hanson

I spent so long feeling frustrated about my years at school. Although my school was not outwardly homophobic, the uncomfortable silence and the eagerness to push all matters relating to gender and sexuality to the side within the school grounds was deafening to me. Over thirteen years, not one class was dedicated to LGBTIQ identity. The only time I heard the word "gay" was when it was thrown around as a slur in the schoolyard.

This frustration manifested in a lot of ways. I became frustrated at my school for failing to implement any services or support that would have made me feel less alone. I became frustrated at my peers for perpetuating the silence. Most importantly, I became frustrated at myself for being different.

In many ways, reading Benjamin Law's *Moral Panic 101* was like opening up a childhood diary or talking to an old friend: raw, therapeutic, comforting. Law takes an admirably level-headed approach to a debate that can understandably send many into a spiral of fumes; admittedly, I've had to calm myself down on the odd occasion for fear of getting too passionate about the subject matter.

As Law suggests, I was one of the readers who was wondering "why so few kids were engaged in a discussion that was, apparently, about their welfare." He is right: there was a lot of speaking for children rather than with children, in a similar way that some debates surrounding marriage equality completely ignore the voices and lived experiences of families with same-sex parents.

The blunt truth is that queer kids are still developing mental illnesses, engaging in self-harm and killing themselves at a glaringly higher rate than that of non-queer kids (you only need to take a brief glance at the National LGBTI Health Alliance's statistics to see this). This is no freakish coincidence.

Only a handful of identities and stories are being shown to children in the school curriculum, meaning that myriad lived experiences aren't being adequately represented. Children deserve to feel represented and valued, both in and out of the classroom, for their differences.

When an issue is politicised, the core intentions can often be forgotten and the original messages can be lost or obscured.

In many ways, Australia is still in denial about the homophobia that occurs here, often blanketed by "other places have it a lot worse" rhetoric. Yet avoidance of and silence around the issue can be just as harmful as direct, overt displays of homophobia, biphobia and transphobia. Prejudice can often be insidious, noticeable only to those who are directly affected.

It's time to give schoolkids more credit: they're more intelligent and evolved than we think. "Sometimes, to our embarrassment and shame," writes Law, "it's adults – not children – who are least equipped to understand, accept or process new realities about the world in which we live." After all, one isn't born with hate or prejudice; it is acquired through lived experience.

We can all take something away from this essay; through his poised writing, Law creates an inviting, inclusive and safe space in which to reflect and discuss. *Moral Panic 101* is a step forward in reconciling the historically tumultuous relationship between gayness and the classroom, creating awareness of the need to modify the school curriculum to promote inclusivity, and advocating for those who still feel silenced by fear. What an important step that is.

It's true: the kids are alright.

Louis Hanson

Benjamin Law

We told you it'd get ugly.

I was finishing writing Moral Panic 101 when the Turnbull Coalition government announced its legally unprecedented, non-binding $122 million same-sex marriage vox pop.[1] Since then, trains have been defaced with anti-gay slogans and swastikas; tyres have been slashed outside a Sydney theatre staging Holding the Man; a News Corp reporter's dog (their dog) was attacked for wearing an Equality scarf; rainbow letterboxes have been defaced and actual shit left on doorsteps; rainbow flags have been ripped from apartments and burned at the door; Kevin Rudd's godson was punched bloody in broad daylight for supporting marriage equality; and a practising GP crowed to an audience that homosexuality is "a disordered form of behaviour." In all of this, the Australian Christian Lobby and Coalition for Marriage – presumably out of desperation – has lied through its collective teeth, telling anyone who'll listen that legalising same-sex marriage in Australia will somehow lead to mandatory "radical" gender education in schools – whatever that means. Yes, there's been ugliness on "both sides," but nowhere near approaching a comparable scale. Forgive your queer friends if they seem bloody tired right now.

If the past few months has achieved anything positive, though, it's been the banding together of LGBTIQ communities, supporters, friends and families. Seeing straight mates gather in parks to cold-call people to vote yes, and my little sisters do a neighbourhood letter-drop (completely unprompted by me), has been galvanising. As Amy Middleton – who is responsible for one of the most consistently interesting and courageous magazines in Australia – notes, "It isn't easy for members of the wider community to put themselves in the shoes of

---

1 It's not a vote, since votes are binding. It's not a plebiscite, as plebiscites in Australian involve mandatory participation; and it's barely a survey, given surveys employ rigorous methods to ensure statistical accuracy. It's a vox pop.

people experiencing oppression." And yet it feels as if these last few months have seen a shift, as Australians now acknowledge and resist a current of homophobia that courses beneath the surface of Australian life, and manifests in its politics.

For me personally, this past quarter has also been a sobering reminder that Australia has a way to go in understanding LGBTIQ people. This isn't just about Australians getting their heads around gender-variance – as I argued in Moral Panic 101 – but same-sex attraction too. At a State Library of NSW discussion of the essay, audience members asked me questions such as: (1) "Where is the medical evidence showing why people are gay?" (2) "Why doesn't Safe Schools cover the higher rates of STDs for men who have sex with each other?" (3) "Why do queer people insist on using the word 'queer'; it's such an ugly word and aren't we all just normal people at the end of the day?" One woman even patiently explained to me that the only reason I was homosexual was because I'd been medically interfered with in utero. This was news to me. And here I was worrying that what I'd written was too remedial.

The concerted campaign to destroy Safe Schools hasn't gone anywhere either. Given much of the commentary has been based on rapid-fire misinformation and fabrication, I'm genuinely grateful for the considered, thorough correspondence to Moral Panic 101. (I also apologise to Senator Scott Ryan for the hiccup about party-room details.) Still, I found some of the responses odd. Dr John Whitehall, for instance, would like to have it both ways. On the one hand, he insists that gender-variance and dysphoria are rare, and that the twenty-eight GPs to whom he's personally chatted haven't encountered much of it. Then he goes on to describe gender-questioning youth as an "epidemic" and "fad." Which is it? Also, doesn't "fad" imply something trendy? As British transgender blogger Mia Violent wryly noted on Twitter, "Soon every parent will be rushing down to the shops to buy their kid the hottest new craze: Painful dysphoria and social ostracisation."

Whitehall keeps digging: "If, for argument's sake, I accept the assertion that 1.2 to 4 per cent of adolescents report being transgender or gender-variant (which I do not) …" Hold up there. Why doesn't Whitehall provide an explanation for why he's rejecting those figures? Why dismiss the findings of a 2013 New Zealand study, reported in the Journal of Adolescent Health, involving 8166 youths, and a 2017 German study of 940 adolescents? They represent literally thousands more people than the anaemic studies Whitehall cites. And why is Whitehall still so reluctant to engage with actual young people? They're kids, not leprechauns. In my experience, they're not hard to find. Since Moral Panic 101 came out, one even became Victoria's Young Australian of the Year.

Louis Hanson reminded me of something I wish I'd emphasised more in *Moral Panic 101*: there doesn't need to be outward homophobia for young people to feel vulnerable at school. Kids and teenagers don't need to be spat on, kicked or beaten up to feel suffocation and a complete absence of support from principals and teachers. To spend your school years completely unacknowledged or accommodated for, and to leave school unequipped for your adult reality – this is the experience of too many. Hanson's reply also made me wish I'd emphasised something else in *Moral Panic 101*: that Safe Schools isn't exclusively beneficial for LGBTIQ youth. Perhaps it's pointing out the obvious, but straight youth cop the blunt effects of homophobia and transphobia too. It's used in the schoolyard to police mannerisms, to define how girls and boys should behave and to keep people in their place. As one recent Canadian study found, schools employing initiatives similar to those recommended by Safe Schools have seen suicides and suicide attempts in British Colombia reduced by 50 per cent – for straight males.

Dennis Altman also astutely picks up on something I wish I'd grasped while writing the essay: the "panic felt by many believing Christians that the world they have known is literally collapsing around them." When I was drafting the essay, one early reader asked me why all this had happened. In the essay, I pointed to several theories: that Safe Schools coverage provided the *Australian* with a handy boost in sales; that it was a useful tool in an ongoing culture war and an emblem of that newspaper's continued political relevance in the face of a fragmenting readership. But Altman is bang-on. What the same-sex marriage "debate" has starkly revealed is the savagery of the Christian hard right and the lengths they'll go to in order to ensure their worldview and moral rectitude is forced on the country, non-believers be damned. The Anglican Archbishop of Sydney, Glenn Davies, was even willing to contribute $1 million to the "No" campaign to that end. Tony Abbott, Miranda Devine, Cory Bernardi, Glenn Davies and co. genuinely see themselves as warriors in some last stand of Christianity in this country.

One of those self-appointed holy warriors, of course, is Lyle Shelton. After the last few months – well, years, really – of hearing Shelton speak, I'm not sure how seriously anyone is supposed to take what he says anymore. It's important to call out Shelton for what he is: a well-groomed, charming peddler of fibs. For the last few months, Shelton has been the frontman for a campaign that has spent countless dollars booking full-page newspaper advertisements telling readers: "A YES VOTE WILL MEAN RADICAL LGBTIQ SEX AND GENDER EDUCATION PROGRAMS ARE COMPULSORY IN OUR KIDS' CLASSROOMS." (Capital letters theirs.) This claim has been repeatedly quashed by sources ranging from Professor Bill Louden (who was responsible for the federal review of Safe Schools) and the ABC's Fact Check. Still, Shelton insists it's the truth.

As the most public face of the "No" campaign, Shelton has conjured the strangest spectres and hypotheticals to spook the Australian voting public into fearing same-sex marriage and Safe Schools. If same-sex marriage is legalised, he says, people will be able to change their legal gender. (People can already do this in Australia.) Shelton also claims that same-sex marriage will lead to mandatory radical gender and sex education. If he's referring to the Safe Schools-developed *All of Us* resource, discussed at length in *Moral Panic 101*, Professor Bill Louden has not only approved that resource but also gone on to definitively debunk Shelton's claim, stating that there "is no link between the federal *Marriage Act* and the Australian Curriculum." Shelton and his colleagues at the Australian Christian Lobby and Coalition of Marriage are many things, but they are not stupid. There can only be one explanation for their repeatedly bearing false witness: they don't have a leg to stand on.

What's been gratifying about writing *Moral Panic 101*, however, has been correspondence from parents. After the *Australian* personally went after me and my Twitter account (a hilarious story, one for another time), one father got in touch to tell me he was initially shocked and offended, then gave me the benefit of the doubt, read the essay and came out feeling more equipped to raise his three sons. Another reader wrote to me about his high-school experience. Although there wasn't explicit homophobic abuse, he did have suicidal thoughts. Once he disclosed to his chaplain that he was gay, the chaplain showed visible disgust and recommended the student medicate himself and never tell anyone. That reader felt compelled to send a copy of *Moral Panic 101* to the current principal of his old high school. I've lost count of the mums and dads who've passed *Moral Panic 101* to other mums and dads, and I am grateful.

By the time you read this, the results on same-sex marriage survey will have been published on the Australian Bureau of Statistics' website, along with a statement on that survey's quality and integrity. If Malcolm Turnbull is true to his word, legislation on same-sex marriage will then go to a conscience vote. Already some conservative politicians have pledged to do everything in their power to prevent this from happening. The process will be protracted, and the unnecessary pain LGBTIQ Australian kids and adults have felt over the past quarter will continue and deepen. And in all of this, both federal and state MPs will continue to deny a timeline of events that's now on the public record, and continue to lie to the public. How arrogant adults can be. How dangerous. How childish.

Benjamin Law

Dennis Altman is emeritus professor of politics at La Trobe University. His most recent book (with Jon Symons) is *Queer Wars*.

Louis Hanson is a writer and LGBTIQ mental-health advocate. He has written for SBS, Fairfax, the *Guardian* and the *Huffington Post*.

Benjamin Law is the author of *Gaysia* and the memoir *The Family Law*, which he adapted for SBS TV. A columnist for Fairfax's *Good Weekend* magazine, Law has written for the *Monthly*, *Frankie*, *QWeekend*, the *Big Issue*, *Crikey* and *Griffith Review*.

Amy Middleton is the founding editor of *Archer Magazine*. She has written for *Australian Geographic*, the *Guardian*, *Rolling Stone*, *Daily Life*, the *Big Issue*, the *Bulletin*, *Junkee*, *Meanjin* and the *Lifted Brow*.

Scott Ryan has been a senator since 2007. He has served as the Special Minister of State since July 2016 and the Minister Assisting the Prime Minister for Cabinet since January 2017.

Lyle Shelton is managing director of the Australian Christian Lobby. He has worked in the press, in Christian ministry, as a Toowoomba city councillor and as political adviser to two Queensland senators.

Hugh White is the author of *The China Choice and Quarterly Essay 39, Power Shift*. He is professor of strategic studies at ANU and has been an intelligence analyst with the Office of National Assessments, a journalist with the *Sydney Morning Herald*, a senior adviser to Defence Minister Kim Beazley and Prime Minister Bob Hawke, and a senior official in the Department of Defence, where from 1995 to 2000 he was deputy secretary for strategy and intelligence, and principal author of Australia's Defence White Paper 2000.

John Whitehall is professor of paediatrics at Western Sydney University.

QUARTERLY ESSAY AUTO-RENEWING SUBSCRIPTIONS NOW AVAILABLE

SUBSCRIBE to Quarterly Essay & SAVE up to 24% on the cover price.

Enjoy free home delivery of the print edition and full digital access on the Quarterly Essay website, iPad, iPhone and Android apps.

FORTHCOMING ISSUE:

Mark McKenna on the Use and Abuse of Australian history March 2018

....

Subscriptions: Receive a discount and never miss an issue. Mailed direct to your door.

☐ **1 year auto-renewing print and digital subscription*** (4 issues): $69.95 within Australia.
Outside Australia $109.95

☐ **1 year print and digital subscription** (4 issues): $79.95 within Australia. Outside Australia $119.95

☐ **1 year auto-renewing digital subscription*** (4 issues): $44.95

☐ **1 year digital only subscription** (4 issues): $49.95

☐ **2 year print and digital subscription** (8 issues): $149.95 within Australia

Gift Subscriptions: Give an inspired gift.

☐ **1 year print and digital gift subscription** (4 issues): $79.95 within Australia. Outside Australia $119.95

☐ **1 year digital only gift subscription** (4 issues): $49.95

☐ **2 year print and digital gift subscription** (8 issues): $149.95 within Australia

All prices include GST, postage and handling. *Your subscription will automatically renew until you notify us to stop. Prior to the end of your subscription period, we will send you a reminder notice.

Please turn over for subscription order form, or subscribe online at **www.quarterlyessay.com**
Alternatively, call 1800 077 514 or 03 9486 0244 or email subscribe@blackincbooks.com

Back Issues: (Prices include GST, postage and handling.)

- ☐ **QE 1** ($15.99) Robert Manne *In Denial*
- ☐ **QE 2** ($15.99) John Birmingham *Appeasing Jakarta*
- ☐ **QE 3** ($15.99) Guy Rundle *The Opportunist*
- ☐ **QE 4** ($15.99) Don Watson *Rabbit Syndrome*
- ☐ **QE 5** ($15.99) Mungo MacCallum *Girt By Sea*
- ☐ **QE 6** ($15.99) John Button *Beyond Belief*
- ☐ **QE 7** ($15.99) John Martinkus *Paradise Betrayed*
- ☐ **QE 8** ($15.99) Amanda Lohrey *Groundswell*
- ☐ **QE 9** ($15.99) Tim Flannery *Beautiful Lies*
- ☐ **QE 10** ($15.99) Gideon Haigh *Bad Company*
- ☐ **QE 11** ($15.99) Germaine Greer *Whitefella Jump Up*
- ☐ **QE 12** ($15.99) David Malouf *Made in England*
- ☐ **QE 13** ($15.99) Robert Manne with David Corlett *Sending Them Home*
- ☐ **QE 14** ($15.99) Paul McGeough *Mission Impossible*
- ☐ **QE 15** ($15.99) Margaret Simons *Latham's World*
- ☐ **QE 16** ($15.99) Raimond Gaita *Breach of Trust*
- ☐ **QE 17** ($15.99) John Hirst *'Kangaroo Court'*
- ☐ **QE 18** ($15.99) Gail Bell *The Worried Well*
- ☐ **QE 19** ($15.99) Judith Brett *Relaxed & Comfortable*
- ☐ **QE 20** ($15.99) John Birmingham *A Time for War*
- ☐ **QE 21** ($15.99) Clive Hamilton *What's Left?*
- ☐ **QE 22** ($15.99) Amanda Lohrey *Voting for Jesus*
- ☐ **QE 23** ($15.99) Inga Clendinnen *The History Question*
- ☐ **QE 24** ($15.99) Robyn Davidson *No Fixed Address*
- ☐ **QE 25** ($15.99) Peter Hartcher *Bipolar Nation*
- ☐ **QE 26** ($15.99) David Marr *His Master's Voice*
- ☐ **QE 27** ($15.99) Ian Lowe *Reaction Time*
- ☐ **QE 28** ($15.99) Judith Brett *Exit Right*
- ☐ **QE 29** ($15.99) Anne Manne *Love & Money*
- ☐ **QE 30** ($15.99) Paul Toohey *Last Drinks*
- ☐ **QE 31** ($15.99) Tim Flannery *Now or Never*
- ☐ **QE 32** ($15.99) Kate Jennings *American Revolution*
- ☐ **QE 33** ($15.99) Guy Pearse *Quarry Vision*
- ☐ **QE 34** ($15.99) Annabel Crabb *Stop at Nothing*
- ☐ **QE 35** ($15.99) Noel Pearson *Radical Hope*
- ☐ **QE 36** ($15.99) Mungo MacCallum *Australian Story*
- ☐ **QE 37** ($15.99) Waleed Aly *What's Right?*
- ☐ **QE 38** ($15.99) David Marr *Power Trip*
- ☐ **QE 39** ($15.99) Hugh White *Power Shift*
- ☐ **QE 40** ($15.99) George Megalogenis *Trivial Pursuit*
- ☐ **QE 41** ($15.99) David Malouf *The Happy Life*
- ☐ **QE 42** ($15.99) Judith Brett *Fair Share*
- ☐ **QE 43** ($15.99) Robert Manne *Bad News*
- ☐ **QE 44** ($15.99) Andrew Charlton *Man-Made World*
- ☐ **QE 45** ($15.99) Anna Krien *Us and Them*
- ☐ **QE 46** ($15.99) Laura Tingle *Great Expectations*
- ☐ **QE 47** ($15.99) David Marr *Political Animal*
- ☐ **QE 48** ($15.99) Tim Flannery *After the Future*
- ☐ **QE 49** ($15.99) Mark Latham *Not Dead Yet*
- ☐ **QE 50** ($15.99) Anna Goldsworthy *Unfinished Business*
- ☐ **QE 51** ($15.99) David Marr *The Prince*
- ☐ **QE 52** ($15.99) Linda Jaivin *Found in Translation*
- ☐ **QE 53** ($15.99) Paul Toohey *That Sinking Feeling*
- ☐ **QE 54** ($15.99) Andrew Charlton *Dragon's Tail*
- ☐ **QE 55** ($15.99) Noel Pearson *A Rightful Place*
- ☐ **QE 56** ($15.99) Guy Rundle *Clivosaurus*
- ☐ **QE 57** ($15.99) Karen Hitchcock *Dear Life*
- ☐ **QE 58** ($15.99) David Kilcullen *Blood Year*
- ☐ **QE 59** ($15.99) David Marr *Faction Man*
- ☐ **QE 60** ($15.99) Laura Tingle *Political Amnesia*
- ☐ **QE 61** ($15.99) George Megalogenis *Balancing Act*
- ☐ **QE 62** ($15.99) James Brown *Firing Line*
- ☐ **QE 63** ($15.99) Don Watson *Enemy Within*
- ☐ **QE 64** ($22.99) Stan Grant *The Australian Dream*
- ☐ **QE 65** ($22.99) David Marr *The White Queen*
- ☐ **QE 66** ($22.99) Anna Krien *The Long Goodbye*
- ☐ **QE 67** ($22.99) Benjamin Law *Moral Panic 101*

☐ I enclose a cheque/money order made out to Schwartz Publishing Pty Ltd.
☐ Please debit my credit card (Mastercard, Visa or Amex accepted).

Card No. ☐☐☐☐ ☐☐☐☐ ☐☐☐☐ ☐☐☐☐

Expiry date / **CCV** **Amount $**

Cardholder's name **Signature**

Name

Address

Email **Phone**

Post or fax this form to: Quarterly Essay, Reply Paid 90094, Carlton VIC 3053 / Freecall: 1800 077 514
Tel: (03) 9486 0288 / Fax: (03) 9011 6106 / Email: subscribe@quarterlyessay.com
Subscribe online at **www.quarterlyessay.com**